PCI DSS Bootcamp The A-Z Information Security Guide

Book Wave Publications

Published by Book Wave Publications, 2024.

Also by Book Wave Publications

How To Make Money In Stocks Value Investing Strategies
Master The Steps To Move Away From The Past And
Following Inspiration
Heartful Journeys: Exploring The Power Of Mindful Living
Essential Computer Networking Concepts You Should Know
Harnessing Your Inner Strength Overcoming Limiting Beliefs
Mastering Networking Basics From Novice To Pro
Mastering Success Harnessing The Hidden Potential Of
Presuppositions
Start Your Own Business, Be Your Own Boss
Passive Income Powerhouse Learn To Set Yourself Up For Life
PCI DSS Bootcamp The A-Z Information Security Guide

Table of Contents

Copyright

PCI DSS Bootcamp: The A-Z™ Information Security Guide

About

The perfect Book to get started with Payment Card Industry Data Security Standard. A detailed understanding of each of the sub-requirements and how they will be assessed is essential for PCI DSS compliance.

It doesn't matter whether you know the payment card industry data security standard, or you are a security professional, this Book will help you to understand the protection of payments in a very effective and simple way! We have tried to explain all the requirements and topics in a very simple way so that you don't have to memorize. We are pretty sure that this is the perfect Book for you to get started in the payments security industry.

Since its formation, PCI DSS has gone through several iterations in order to keep up with changes to the online threat landscape. While the basic rules for compliance have remained constant, new requirements are periodically added.

This Book is a must for every computer user of an organization. No prior training is required to take this Book as we will start with the basics. This will be a major step up in your career so what are you waiting for?

Jump on in and take your career to the next level by learning information security today. I'll see you in the Book!

Introduction

Hello and welcome to Introduction to Fraud Prevention. In this Book we are going to cover everything related to fraud, payment, fraud and specifically who does it, what techniques are used to prevent it, how to assemble a strategy and what more. Let's take a moment to cover the topics and goals for this Book. Hello and welcome to Introduction to Fraud Prevention, where we are going to cover everything related to how to identify fraud and actually prevent it. In this Book, our main goal is to cover the fundamentals of how fraud is both performed, but also preventive. We are going to touch on many different topics, including just for example, which types of actors actually perform fraud, as well as the motivations that each one has and how they actually execute it, or what are the different executions of fraud. And what they have in common as well is how they are usually detected.

The different patterns will also cover, for example, an exhaustive list in, I mean, exhaustive of fraud prevention techniques that validate transaction data identities. And for this purpose, use methods ranging from technology to human processes and much more. Or for example, which combination of fraud prevention techniques at the end of the day forms the optimal system to monitor and prevent fraud for each individual organization. How do you pick it and how do you optimize it? Back to the Book structure. In order to cover everything related to fraud prevention, we are going to split this Book into three key chapters. The first is about the actual approaches to fraud.

In short, how fraud is performed, who does it, what fraud strategies look like in general, and how specific executions differ. After that, we'll cover actual fraud prevention techniques, the tools which are used as part of a bigger system to actually prevent fraud. Each technique usually validates a specific data point or multiple, and we are going to cover all the different types of techniques possible. And finally, we'll cover the fraud prevention strategy itself. It is how do they define a general strategy for your company based on all the specific techniques that we mentioned, how to pick them, how to put them together, as well as how to optimize that solution in terms of people and data. So as you see, this is what we're going to cover in this Book. Who does fraud, how to prevent it with techniques, and how to assemble a long term solution.

Fraud Fundamentals

Let's cover some fundamentals of fraud. That is, before we dive into the topics. It's especially important to define what are the basics, what is payment fraud, how does it occur? Who is the victim and more? Payment fraud is a global problem and it's only expected to become worse as time goes by. Google losses from payment fees have tripled from around 10 billion in 2011 to around 32 billion in 2020. So they have more than tripled and they are expected to grow 25% more to around 40 billion in 2027. Payment fraud is a risk for multiple stakeholders. It's a risk for online merchants as well as their banks, the merchant banks or acquiring banks. This is because the merchant owes money from shops instead of their banks in the chargeback process.

Consumers in transactions also lose, especially if they're a victim of fraud themselves as well as the banks that issue their cards. The issuing bank's fraud risk is a type of risk that is very different from others. With me elaborate. There are usually three major risks in a banking institution. The first is attrition risk. This is the risk of losing clients, especially in competitive environments with a lot of other banks. The second is credit risk. It's the risk of a client of the bank just not paying on time. And the third is fraud risk. This is the risk of fraud occurring on their clients accounts. So while both attrition and credit risk can be managed in estimates and they can be considered the cost of doing business fraud, the risk is different.

It requires close monitoring. It can't be properly estimated and it constantly changes. It's also important to clarify the differences between fraud and disputes. Fraud is actually a type of dispute or to be more correct. Fraud causes one type of dispute between a merchant and the consumer. There may be other disputes besides fraud, but fraud causes one of them. Disputes usually originate from four major problem types. The first is fraud. As we just mentioned, someone impersonated a customer or stole their information. The second type are authorization issues. The consumer did not allow the merchant to charge this value or the authorisation is not clear. The third type of disputes are processing errors.

The merchant provides the wrong information or uses the wrong API, automates the transaction, expires or other processing problems. And the last type of disputes are consumer disputes. The consumer claims that the product is faulty or fake or was not the way or others. A dispute usually occurs when a consumer requests a chargeback of the transaction value, and usually the reason code provided by the card issuer like Visa or MasterCard reflects that specific dispute type. The reason code is a database field that, when communicated, will state very explicitly the reason for the chargeback. So for example, if it's a fraud code, it will state whether it's a liability shift issue, a like merchant or another reason.

What are some examples of fraud trends and context nowadays? The first is identity theft. One of the most pervasive types of drop. The perpetrator takes control of all information necessary to impersonate a person. It's hard to detect if there is a distinction between automatic and manual. Some fraud cases are handled automatically and some are handled manually. For example, if your credit card number is a blacklisted or hot twisted, which is a synonym in the fraud world, then the transaction is automatically rejected. In other cases that may be more complex, then a manual review is necessary. Then we have chargebacks. Chargeback is the term used to describe a request for the money to be returned to a consumer.

It has costs for both banks and merchants, and it should be avoided. It's important to realize that a chargeback doesn't just return the value of the transaction to the consumer, but it actually has associated fees for the bank and for the merchant. So even fraud cases that are solved don't have a zero result. They can still result in losses. What are our key takeaways here? The first is that fraud is a problem for everyone. It's a risk for both merchants and consumers into the banks of both fraud. Risk is hard to predict. Every chargeback has an additional cost. There are different types of risks, especially for banks.

But like attrition, risk or credit risk, fraud risk is not easy to measure at all, and it requires constant attention and vigilance due to its fluid nature. Finally, disputes in front are not synonyms. There are multiple reasons for dispute, and fraud is one of those reasons. Not all disputes are due to France, but every detective's fraud case always causes a dispute. So as we see, fraud is a big problem. It's a type of risk that, unlike other types of risk, cannot be predicted. And it can be a big problem for both merchants and consumers and their respective banks.

Fraud Approaches Intro

We are now at the Fraud Approaches chapter. In this chapter, we are going to cover how fraud is actually committed in specific payment fraud. We are going to cover the general executions, the specific executions and the people who do it. Let's take a look at the topics for this chapter. Welcome to the Fraud Approaches chapter. In this chapter, we will cover the different strategies and executions of fraud by different actors in terms of progress. We are at the first chapter. Three in this chapter will cover how fraud is actually performed and by whom. Both the general strategies, but also the specific implementations.

In the second chapter, we'll cover the different types of fraud prevention techniques: hotlist, velocity checks, information verification tokens and devices and many others. And finally, in the third chapter, we'll cover strategy design, what a fraud prevention strategy entails and how to optimize one. What are our goals for this chapter? Well, our major goal is to know more about the people who commit fraud and how to do it. It includes, for example, the following topics: the different types of fraud strategy, defining how the information itself is gathered in how it's used. For example, obtaining information for social engineering through internal fraud, through identity theft or other means. Then the specific executions of fraud from using a card lock generator to cash return from internal firms and others.

And finally, who are the different types of perpetrators and their motivations from end consumers to hackers to white collar agents, organized criminals and others in terms of fraud approaches? We will be covering three major topics in specific. The first are the general strategies how fraudsters collect and use information from a bird's eye point of view. Then the specific execution times. How FAR is actually performed to a deep level, usually in one of six major ways. And finally, who are the different perpetrator types? Consumers, hackers, criminals, and others. So as we see, we are going to cover three groups of topics in this chapter. The general approaches the specific executions and the perpetrators.

General Strategies: Intro

Let's take a look at the general strategy. That is, what are the top level approaches that fraudsters use to obtain information that they will then leverage in specific executions? It can be grabbing credit cards from someone due to convenience. It can be internal fraud where you obtain information from the company that you work for and others. So let's take a look. Let's cover the general strategies. Fraud perpetrators usually employ one of a few major strategies to collect information and use it. Despite the specific executions, which can be consumer fraud card work for many others, the ways that information is actually obtained in use themselves are mostly the same, and they can be grouped into a few major types. Four of them in specific.

We are going to cover how fraudsters obtain information for social engineering by leveraging easily accessible credit card information in other general strategies. In specific, we are going to take a look at the four major types of general strategies. The first is convenience. Also known as ease of use. In other words, someone commits fraud because they can easily obtain a credit card in the real world, or they have easy access to information that can be used for fraud. It's quick and easy to use. The second type is social engineering, which consists of manipulating someone into giving you personal information that you can then use to impersonate them or commit fraud or others. The third type is internal fraud.

This is when an internal actor of a company leaks information from that company to someone else so that they can commit fraud or they do it themselves. This can be to either hurt the company or help the particular person. Sometimes both. And finally, identity theft. The most dangerous time. It consists of obtaining enough information to actually impersonate a person. It can be very hard to detect. So as you see, there are several general strategies for obtaining the information. It can be from someone else, stealing their identity from a company just because it's convenient or more. And we are going to cover every one of these.

General Strategies: Convenience

Let's talk about convenience fraud, for lack of a better description. This is fraud which is committed because it's easy to do. For example, you install a machine on an ATM or a post terminal and you immediately have access to hundreds or thousands of credit cards per day. They are easy to access. Let's take a look at convenience fraud in more detail. Convenience fraud is very simple. It consists of using readily available information that can then be used for fraud. It's very frequent in situations where the fraudster has access to a lot of different information from many different people. For example, being a retail or a restaurant worker which allows them to easily test the details of multiple cards or people.

This type of fraud also includes the known technique of skimming, where the person gathers credit card information and actually copies the cards, replicating the magnetic strip or the chip. So the fraudster can start by impersonating a retail worker or actually being one, then gathering credit card information such as gathering the numbers or actually planting a mechanism known as the skimmer that gathers the information itself. When the card, the swipe, this can be planted in any retailer's point of sale or at an actual ATM to gather card information in mass. In the case of ATMs, it's usually accompanied by a camera to gather the person's pin as well by filming them. The convenience approach.

The fraud allows the perpetrator to easily test many different types of cards to check which transactions are walkable, or, in other words, which cards have institutions that are well-protected and which ones aren't, and allows them to check what is the low hanging fruit that can be exploited later? Then the fraudster can go deeper on those cards whose banks are the least protected against fraud? It's almost like a test. A high number of them and the ones that pass the test continue to be used. For example, it's very common for a fraudster to skim information on 50 different cards in a day or a lot more. In the case of organized criminals, then they test all of them with small false purchases, and then they use the ones that are not immediately blocked or flagged for bigger and bigger transactions.

What are some examples of convenience from? The first is ATM skimmers. Fraudsters can place skimmers in ATMs and discover the card slot and pretend to be another card slot on top of the actual one. The person doesn't realize, but they act as an intermediary that passes the card to both the inside and the outside, but copies the number. In the meantime, the second example is retail workers. One of the most frequent types of credit card skimming occurs in retail, where someone uses a skimmer to skim the credit card information or actually notes it down or photographs it. Naturally, only a few select retail workers perform froth. Most are honest, but I'm just saying that this is the perfect breeding ground for skimming from in.

Finally, we have something called shimmers. So skimmers, no, they don't work because they are based on cards that are used with just the magnetic strip. But nowadays, most cards use Chip instead. So the introduction of chip cards made a lot of skimmers pretty much useless. So fraudsters created new devices called shimmers, and instead of working through the magnetic strip, actually worked through the chip card. They're the equivalent of skimmers. But for chip cards, what are our key takeaways here? The first is that convenience fraud relies on the information being easy to test.

This approach relies on having ready access to multiple credit card information so that the fraudster can test, which allows deeper froth and going deeper with those. One of the most known types of convenience fraud is skimming obtaining credit card information, either by noting it down, photographing it, or using a mechanism so that then this number can either be used digitally or an actual copy of the card can be made to use with a magnetic strip. Skimming amongst fraudsters to collect a lot of different credit card numbers in a short amount of time in high traffic areas. And finally, convenience fraud is usually an approach. It is a gateway to other types of fraud.

The goal of the fraudster is to use this as kind of a testbed to discriminate which cards are the most vulnerable and which institutions are the least protected. And then they can allow other approaches for fraud on the cards that are the. Most vulnerable. So as we see, convenience fraud is very popular because the credit cards are easy to test and it's usually a gateway, that is, you obtain a large volume of credit cards, you test which ones are easy to further leverage, and then you leverage those.

General Strategies: Social Engineering

Let's talk about social engineering. Social engineering consists of pretending to be someone else, usually with already a part of the information that you're supposed to have. Didn't give the person to give you the rest of the information. For example, calling, pretending to be from the security team or from the bank and saying, hey, we have a security problem. You really need to give me your password or your credit card number. But there are other ways to do social engineering. What's the goal of social engineering? Put simply, it is the practice of manipulating someone into revealing confidential information. The name says you are engineering them using specific social skills to accomplish your goal.

It's frequently used by the fraudster pretending to be someone that they are not usually part of the security team of some institution related to the person. There are usually two major approaches to actual social engineering. The first one is over the phone conversations impersonating an employee. This is, for example, calling someone at a company and saying, Hey, this is John from the Security Department. We've had a problem with some of our accounts. Can you please confirm your current password? The second example that has become more and more relevant is phishing. It consists of sending false emails, SMSes, or even creating a fake website so that a user will think that they're dealing with a trusted institution or bank in actually sharing personal data with them.

Social engineering, in most cases, relies on using existing information that the perpetrator knows about the person in order to appear to be illegitimate. This makes the person assume that they are in fact who they claim to be, and it makes it easier for them to reveal more information. If you pretend to be a member of the security team, it's easier to ask for their passwords if you already know their full name and address and maybe the start date for the job and you repeat it back to them first. It gives off the impression that you're supposed to have that information. So, for example, someone impersonating a company employee can obtain what is called open source, intelligent, aware, sent on the person such as their position in start date from their LinkedIn profile and possibly other elements such as their address, their spouse name, their children names and others from Facebook.

Then when you call the person you state, John, just to confirm, you have this in this position with this and they start to date this or this address, maybe more details. So I have the right account right then to confirm. And then you say, okay, so we've had a problem with some of our accounts. Can you please share your password with me? What are some examples of social engineering? The first is banking communications. One of the most common types of phishing is false communications from banking institutions asking you to confirm your pin, your password or other confidential information. Then social networks. A variation of these are false communications from Facebook or other social networks, asking you to confirm your password or other confidential details.

In many cases, these don't give the person enough information for fraud, but it gives them enough confidential information for them to pretend to be a security expert and then call the person to do even more. Social engineering. And in this case, the perpetrator even knows that they easily fall prey to this kind of maneuver. And finally, calls from security teams, as we mentioned, the original type of social engineering, calling someone in a company and claiming to be from the security team and asking for their password. Sounds so basic, but it's so frequent and surprisingly, it has a very high success rate. What are our key takeaways here? The first is that social engineering is nothing more than manipulating others into giving you personal or confidential information.

And usually you do it by pretending to be someone legitimate that may already have some of their information. Then social engineering is usually performed by leveraging existing information about the person. The more that you show that you already know about them, the more easily you can obtain even more information. And finally, phishing. One of the main types of social engineering is phishing, which consists of sending false information, pretending to be a bank or corporation or others, and, as the name says, phishing for information. Some people will believe this and provide that information. So social engineering, as the name says. Is all about engineering people in specific. And usually you leverage some existing information to seem to have credibility to then get the rest of the information from the person themselves.

General Strategies: Internal Fraud

Let's talk about internal fraud. Internal fraud consists of using information from the company it works for or getting somebody else to do it for you and then using that internal data to commit fraud. Let's take a look. Internal fraud consists of leveraging proprietary information that you or an accomplice has access to from your company internally to commit fraud. It may include, among other examples, belonging to the actual fraud management division of a merchant or retailer in having intimate knowledge of the fraud detection rules and reviewing those to a crime ring in order to let them bypass it. Another example is belonging to the customer support group of a retailer. In knowing which types of chargebacks are automatically approved, in which are contested, to allow fraudsters to buy with stolen credit cards.

In return, the products for cash without any questions or any other situation where internal information is used to facilitate fraud, either by the same person or by a third party. This can be one of the most difficult types to detect precisely because the fraudster knows exactly how to avoid detection in the first place. Internal problems can be grouped into one of two major categories. The first is first party fraud. In other words, the actual consumer performs from the same person that obtains the information, or so commits fraud. So if you are an employee of a company you leverage their return policy to buy products themselves and then use them and then return them without any question. You are doing this. Then we have third party fraud. In this case, if you are the internal actor, you don't commit fraud. You sell information for other fraudsters to use in usually obtaining it in the process.

For example, you can show information about cash returns during the holiday season, which is usually a period that has less strict rules because so many people are returning things. And so information on those rules to a crime ring and make a deal to obtain a kickback of 10% on all fraudulent returns performed for cash. This type of approach is usually done at scale with multiple transactions of small value. The reason for this is that most high value transactions that originate disputes are generally manually reviewed, but the low value ones aren't. So it's especially useful for fraudsters to know the rules around the low value transactions so that they can commit fraud with all situations being automatically handled. So the fraud is never reviewed in the first place. What are some examples of internal troughs? The first time is the fraudulent purchase of offensive items.

An internal agent can sell information on how to detect fraud to a crime ring. And the crime ring can then buy sensible items such as jewels, electronics or digital purchases without being detected. And then sell those for cash. Then we have corporate fraud. An internal agent that knows about return policies can leverage them to buy products from that corporation with a fake account in or leverage the rules to obtain returns without any questions. Another example is insurance fraud. If an internal insurance analyst knows about the investigation protocols, they can allow the person themselves or others to perform insurance fraud because they know exactly what types of rules they can avoid. So in this case, it can be first or third party fraud.

What are our key takeaways here? The first is that internal fraud, as the saying goes, consists of knowing your enemy. It's based on using internal knowledge, especially about fraud, the tension to not be detected when performing fraud. Then it can be first or third person. Internal front can be done directly by the person who knows the internal information or facilitated to other agents who can act on that information. And finally, it has multiple uses. Internal fraud can be used to buy festival items for cash return from corporate fraud many other times, as long as it depends on internal information. So as we see, internal fraud can be there in the first person or third person and for multiple purposes. But what defines it is using internal information to actually commit fraud.

General Strategies: Identity Theft

Let's talk about identity theft. As the name says, this consists of obtaining parts of documentation that represent a person's identity. And usually it's progressive. For example, obtaining identity documents to create a bank account in the person's name and using that bank account in the person's name to then obtain a credit card and so on. It can be very pervasive. And if it's well, then the person can really become indistinguishable from the actual person. White sticker identity theft can be a type of approach where the fraudster obtains enough personal information regarding the person to later be used to impersonate them, as the name says. They literally steal their identity. It's also usually done by layers.

So the fraudster usually uses the existing information to obtain even more information and do that successively until they can perfectly replicate the full person's identity, including bank accounts, documents and more. The information itself can come from multiple sources. The first is by digging through mail or trash in order to obtain personal documents, such as, for example, bills for address verification. The second is by physically stealing wallets or purses, which may have ID documents, for example. The third type is by obtaining personnel records, for example, from co-workers in a company. Another type is skimming information from an ATM, which can include the credit card information.

But more than that, some of the operations that were performed in the ATM, including other account numbers, recent transactions and more in another type, is by actually buying electronic records on the black market or accessing those exposed during data breaches. Malicious hackers known as crackers usually perform data dumps of a successful hack for the public or sell that information in private. It's important to notice that despite most people thinking that the Internet is where most identity theft originated, 90% of it actually comes from other sources such as real world documents or personnel records. Identity theft originates the most dangerous types of fraud because in many cases the fraudster can and does leverage the existing information to then obtain more information on the person.

In many cases, it creates a sort of perfect picture, a perfect replica of their identity that cannot be detected as fraudulent. So, for example, they start by having the person's I.D. and possibly credit card, maybe a bill with their address. This can be used to call the bank and actually change the address and the phone numbers of their account, or even create a new account without them knowing. This can then be used to avoid being flagged in new transactions with enough sophistication. Fraudsters performing identity theft can perform fraud off for a long time, possibly months or years without even being detected in the first place. What are some examples of identity theft? The first is good old dumpster diving.

This is one of the most chapteric types of information gathering in the fraud world, and it consists of, as the name says, perusing someone's trash to find sensitive documents such as bank records, receipts, salary records or other confidential documents. Sophisticated fraudsters can perform unbelievable techniques such as pretending to be job interviewers or real estate agents or car rental agents in order to obtain personal documents from people that they can later use for fraudulent purposes. And finally, phishing. Although this is a type of social engineering, it's also, in many cases, the beginning of identity theft. The fraudster can pretend to be a bank or an institution requesting personal information that they would then use to obtain even more information later.

What are our key takeaways here? The first is that identity theft is a strategy that consists of obtaining personal information from someone in order to later impersonate them. It's usually a dangerous progression. The fraudster can use existing information to progressively obtain more and more until in many cases they reach a perfect impersonation which renders them indistinguishable from the actual person, which is what they want. There are several approaches that aren't compatible with identity theft. The person can fish for information online. They can retrieve it physically. They can impersonate someone else in the first place, among others.

So as we see IDEntity theft usually consists of obtaining personal elements of information to pretend to be another person, and you can obtain them for the internet by standardizing other ways in the real world in many different ways. And usually remember that it's progressive. That is, the fraudster uses the existing information to obtain more information. In fact, that fake identity.

Specific Executions: Intro

Let's talk about specific executions. So far, we've covered the general strategies for obtaining information and committing fraud. But now we are going to cover the specific executions that are new, generate a block of card numbers, do try to commit fraud as a consumer by stating that you didn't receive your product when you did or many other approaches. Let's take a look. Once the information is obtained through one of the few major strategies that we've covered, it comes time to actually commit fraud. Here is where the actual execution of this fraud can vary greatly if several of these types can be used at the same time. There are methods that rely on using a card a single time, multiple times on your own account, using fake accounts.

If you read accounts in many other different variations, these executions, however, can be grouped into six major types, which we'll cover, as mentioned. We'll cover these six key types of fraud execution. The first is consumer froth. This one is usually done by end consumers themselves, and it requires no technology and or skills. It consists of claiming that you didn't receive a product or that it was damaged or other similar reasons. When the product is fine. It's just tricking a merchant. Another type is card fraud. This is when a fraudster generates multiple combinations of credit card numbers and tries them all to see which ones work. And the ones that do work are then saved to make more purchases. It's kind of a spray and pray approach. Then we have single use from a difficult type to detect.

Here you take so much automation for one credit card and you make one single purchase with it. That's it. This minimizes the chances of being caught. Some fraudsters make just one purchase. Others make one purchase per retailer in multiple retailers. Then we have a very simple cash return. You buy a product with a stolen card and then you physically return it in exchange for cash. After that, we have both collusive and affiliate fraud. Two types of internal fraud, inclusive fraud and internal actors. As the name says, they collude with a criminal and they partner up to use internal information for fraud. For example, leaking fraud detection rules so that criminals can now avoid them.

If you read, fraud is similar, but it consists of an internal person setting up an affiliate account and then using stolen credit cards to make purchases that give their account affiliate commissions. And finally, we have the most dangerous type dynamic or tested from. This is usually only done by criminal organizations. In this type of fraud, that information changes constantly, not allowing static rules to catch it in. It requires evolution of the fraud monitoring system to actually keep up with it, but it keeps changing in real time. So as you see in this group of topics, we are going to cover super specific executions of fraud by different actors.

Specific Executions: Consumer Fraud

Talk about consumer fraud. Consumer fraud is very simple. It consists of the consumer trying to lie to the retailer by claiming that a product is effective or you didn't get it. Or any other situation that allows them to get an advantage. For example, obtaining a refund without needing to return the original product which the consumer fraud occurs when the consumer of a product or service themselves are performing from this can take multiple different forms. For example, claiming to not have received the product. When you have in all transaction information claims that you did or are using a product and then returning it later, usually claiming that it was damaged or became damaged afterwards, or claiming that you're not satisfied with a product, returning them while claiming that the product was faulty or misrepresented or counterfeit or just not satisfying.

The common characteristics of this type of fraud is that all transaction information will seem valid in point to a successful purchase. In the only formation it will be out of place is the consumer's information. In this type of fraud. All consumer information will be checked out because the account is real. This means that their address, their phone, their credit card number and all other types of information will be valid. Recommendations to deal with this type of fraud includes first using additional identity checks, such as you were trying to buy signatures or out of pocket checks, which is calling the consumer and asking them questions about their transaction history. In many cases, not even to verify their identity, know it's them, but it's just for non repudiation to tie the person explicitly to this purchase so that they can the night later.

Then using warm waists or hot twists where warm lists are raised of consumers that are flagged but authorized in hot lists are lists of consumers that are walk, for example, taking a consumer that makes an unjustified return, putting them in the warm list, and then the next time they do it, they get placed in the hot list. So if they make too many returns or claim non reception too many times their flag is brand. Another example is having automated chargeback policies, automatic approval, for example, approving every single chargeback below $20. This is because otherwise manual verification and just allocating an analyst to verify these will cost more than the actual product value.

What are some examples of consumer shops? The first is satisfaction from consumer satisfaction from in specific occurs when the consumer claims that the product is defective or not, what they ordered or similar when they're just not satisfied with it. Non reception occurs when the consumer claims that the product that was ordered was never received. When all tracking information points to the contrary and finally successful returns are another example. For example, someone constantly ordering and returning an item such as a chapter game, always within 15 to 30 days so that they can use it in the meantime, but then returning them, claiming that they are defective. What are our key takeaways here? The first is that consumer fraud, unsurprisingly, is perpetrated.

There are no hackers or no criminals involved. The actual buyer is the one performing fraud, the either queen to not be satisfied not having received the item or other variations of this. Second, this type of fraud is easily identifiable because everything else checks out. Nothing in the system flags in this transaction is fraud and only the consumer's opinion or action differs from the data. And finally, it's repetitive by nature. Consumer shops usually involve multiple uses. The person claims that he didn't receive something in multiple cases or they're not satisfied in multiple cases.

And so one which is why hot wastes in warm wastes are so effective in stopping it, they only get two or three chances and afterwards they are blocked. So as we see, consumer fraud can be detected by the fact that everything on paper says that the product was the way or that it's in good condition. In all the testimony of the consumer is something which is different from those facts. It can be easily stopped, these repeat offenses, and at the end of the day, it doesn't do a lot of damage in most cases.

Specific Executions: Card Block Fraud

Let's talk about the card. What does the name say? This consists of randomly generating a block of credit card numbers, usually filtering them to be correct ones, and then testing them to check if the bank has a lot of security measures or not at all, and then usually exploiting the ones with the weakest security measures. What the card looks for occurs when a perpetrator uses a credit card number generator to generate, as the name says, a block of credit card numbers. Usually they have something in common, such as, for example, the bin or a bank identification number. This is represented by the first six digits of a card number, and you can derive further card numbers from this.

So what happens is the fraudster generates these numbers and then they test all of the numbers and they use the valid ones to perform purchases. Usually they do one purchase per card to make sure that the number works in the first place. And once they identify successful numbers, they exploit them further. From a programming point of view. It's almost similar to a password cracker. The fraudster has multiple combinations for the credit card number and they just brute force their way into some of the work and then they make use of those. This type of fraud usually targets smaller banks that are not up to date on identity verification methods, including address verification or card security schemes such as the three digits on the back.

So let's say, for example, that you generate 500 card numbers in the bank for some of these cards. Doesn't require you to use this usual number in order to make a purchase, but the bank for others does. So how easily can you exploit the cards that don't need the CCB number? Chances are very easy so fraudsters can task large quantities of card numbers effectively, and they can identify the cards that have the weakest security and then leverage those in this type of drive. You see a behavior consisting of the same cards being used multiple times with different names for numbers and addresses, especially across retailers. This is because the fraudster has the card number, but they never have the actual name or address of the person.

So you will see the same card number associated with different account information, different names, different phones and so on. Additionally, the person will use false shipping addresses such as a drop off point because they're not sending the purchase to the actual cardholder's home, but the temporary addresses where they can pick up the goods and possibly fast them later. So protection against this type of fraud usually starts with techniques such as velocity of use and velocity of change. Velocity of use is about detecting how many times something is used within a period of time, such as the card number. If it's used very high, it has high velocity and it may be this type of attack and also the velocity of change, or in other words, how frequently a type of information changes within a given time period.

So for this attack, you'll see a high velocity of use for the card number, but a high velocity of change for the phone number or the address or the name, possibly address. Verification is also a powerful measure here because the address used never matches the cardholders. So if you compare the shipping address of the order with an actual address that the cardholder has on file on their bank and they don't match, that's a red flag. What are some examples of cards? The first is generating multiple numbers in brute force, forcing the small retailer's website with all of them.

This is usually the first line of attack in a strategy like this when picking weak banks in retailers is very frequent. If the fraudster knows in advance which retailer doesn't perform verifications, and if they know that the card numbers generated belong to an unprotected bank, they can invest more heavily on the attack because the chance of success will be higher. Another example is physically printing the cards. In the past, before chip card technology, fraudsters could find valid credit card numbers and literally print new cards with them with a magnetic strip, replicate it so that they could test the credit cards. In the real world, not just digitally, but chip technology has made this approach kind of obsolete. What are our key takeaways here? The first is that the card walk fraud consists of generating lots of credit card numbers and then testing them in mass to find winners, both having cards in them.

Belonging to unprotected banks and testing the transactions on unprotected retailers helped this process. Then everything except the card information will be different because the fraudster only knows the credit card number. So on retailer websites you will see the same credit card associated with different names, different phones, and maybe different addresses. Also, velocity techniques work very well here because of how card numbers are used for several small purchases across retailers. Checking the same number with varying address, name or phone number is a good way to detect this type of fraud. So as we see, card fraud consists of generating a high quantity of credit card numbers and then testing them. It is easy to identify because all of the information on file is different. Not the same address, not the same name, just the same number.

Specific Executions: Single-Use Fraud

Let's talk about single use fraud. Yes. The name says this type of fraud consists of using a credit card number only once. It can be once in the fraudsters lifetime or once per merchant. And usually it's hard to detect because you can find a pattern whether you find fraud for this credit card number, yes or no. There are going to be other different numbers and this one will not be used again. Let's take a look at how it works. Single use fraud, as the name says, consists of using a card a single time, maybe a single time for one merchant or a single time per merchant with multiple ones. It's a type that is hard to detect because there is only one single transaction. Wait, a given card? So you have only one data point for analysis. There are multiple approaches that are compatible with this type of fraud.

As long as the card is only used once, for example, the information can be obtained for social engineering. It can be stolen from internal records obtained by perusing trash or mail. Or the numbers can even be generated with a block generator itself. As long as you only use the card once this type of fraud is usually done for highly feasible goods or for cash returns. So transactions where the fraudster can obtain cash immediately, which is one transaction. Jewels, consumer electronics, industry, gaming and supply. The account information here may be valid or not, depending on the general approach, so it may be different in the case of a January of card number because they only have the number and all of the other information is fake or it may be fully valid.

In the case of identity theft, the name, address and everything will match up. But the one thing in common is that delivery addresses will always be different, which will usually be a drop off point for the fraudster to collect the item and convert it to cash. This type of fraud can be detected with velocity of change and velocity of use checks, but it has to be for multiple merchants. Whatever fraud monitoring system you adopt is not going to detect it if it just monitors one merchant. In short, if the fraudster uses one card to make a purchase on Amazon. Another for Walmart. Another for Target. All online. Then a frog monitoring solution that includes all of these can stop it.

But a fraud monitoring solution that only takes into account. Amazon, for example, will never be aware of the other transactions and may not stop them. Another thing that can help is setting up business rules for transaction values or feasible goods on the first transaction. For example, a first time client can't buy more than $50 of jewels on their first purchase. Maybe on the second one they can buy 200. And so on. This can limit good orders, but it prevents this type of fraud. What are some examples of single use fraud? First, a single purchase of jewels, someone using a stolen credit card to purchase jewels from an online retailer to send them to a drop off point, collect them and then finance them for money.

A similar example is buying electronic coins, bitcoin or any other using a stolen credit card to purchase bitcoin, then sending it anonymously to the fraudster his wallet as a transfer, and then possibly reselling it online for cash. And finally, single cash returns. Also work using a stolen credit card to buy a flat screen TV during the holiday season, then sending it to a drop off point, picking it up and then taking it to the retailer physically for a cash return on the spot. This is another example. What are our key takeaways here? The first is that single use fraud, unsurprisingly, consists of using a stolen credit card number to make one single purchase. It can be just one purchase in one retailer or one purchase per retailer in multiple.

It's hard to detect. It's almost impossible if the fraudster only makes one purchase in one retailer because there's only one data point to consider in the case of multiple retailers. It can be possible, as I mentioned. Whatever fraud monitoring system should monitor multiple merchants that system can use. Velocity checks, velocity of use and velocity of change to detect this type of fraud. But it has to consider the multiple merchants being targeted. It's very hard to track with just one. So as we see this type of fraud consists of only using a credit card number once in the person's lifetime or once per retailer, and it's very hard to detect. In the West, merchants are pulling their resources together and the fraud detection solution takes all of them into account.

Specific Executions: Cash Return Fraud

It's like cash written in frost. As the name says, this consists of using a stolen credit card to buy something and then returning it in the real world for cash. For example, using a stolen credit card to buy the PlayStation five for 500 bucks. You'll be lucky if it's only 500 bucks, but then returning it in the real world for those $500. And if you scale this with multiple purchases, the fraudster can easily obtain a large amount of cash with stolen card numbers. Let's take a look at how it works in more detail. The concept of cash return fraud is very simple. One or more purchases are made that are then returned for cash in a real world location. For example, buying a TV online, then going to the physical retailer and returning it for cash due to the nature of this fraud.

It's very present during the holiday season because it's common for people to return gifts during this time without having a receipt, or at least to have to provide less information in order to return them. For example, usually you only get a return in terms of money to the bank account of the credit card that was used for the purchase. But during the holiday season, because someone else buys the gift. It is common to give people the money back in cash. And this is why the holiday season is so targeted. There are multiple strategies that employees execute so the information can be obtained from identity theft, social engineering or others, and all of them are compatible as long as the purchases are made for the purpose of returning the product for cash.

It's also interesting to note that I did not categorize this as a consumer shop for one reason, because usually this is not done by consumers. What I mean is if you buy a product for $20 and you get the cash back as $20, you don't win anything as a consumer. So this type of fraud is usually not performed by consumers, but by crime rates. They take stolen credit cards and get the money back from those purchases. In this case, the account information for the purchase may match the card holders or not. Again, it depends on how it was obtained. In the case of identity theft, all cardholder information can be the same credit cards, phone address, etc..

If it was a January card number, for example, most of it will not match and so on. Once again, one element that's always common is that the delivery address is not the cardholder's. It will usually be a drop off point where the fraudster can pick up the product and return it for cash. This type of fraud can be tackled in multiple ways. One way is for the retailer to have a policy of only providing returns to the original card number. This is very frequent. So regardless of who does the actual return, the money back will always be provided to the bank account of the card and it renders this fraud useless.

You can also use velocity of use and change checks because you are going to see the same cards being used for different purchases in different retailers and in many cases with the same delivery address. And if possible, also using cardholder address verification. In short, if the shipping address doesn't match the actual address for the cardholder, then you block the transaction. What are some examples of cash returned from? Well, attacks done during the holidays are a good example. You can buy items to be returned for cash during this period, especially customer electronics and toys. Then leveraging weak retailer policies. As we stated, some retailers are sophisticated and they only allow returns via a chargeback to the cardholder's card.

These will render fraud impossible, but some retailers can provide gift cards with the item's value or even provide actual cash. These can be and usually are leveraged by fraudsters. In the end, only doing this for transactions with low dollar values is common. This type of fraud is usually performed on a large scale with multiple retailers with items that have low dollar values because high dollar transactions usually require more verifications and more checks. So you won't see this type of fraud with one transaction for a $2,000 MacBook, but you will see it for thousands of transactions for $10 gift cards. What are our key takeaways here? First, cash return fraud simply consists of buying items that can be then returned for cash. Very basic.

Then it takes advantage of retailer policies. Some are more sophisticated and they don't allow for cash returns and some are not sophisticated. And these are the ones that the fraudsters are going to target. And finally. The holiday season is the paradise of cash return because retailers are overloaded and they have to relax their verifications for returns. So this is precisely when criminals leverage this type of fraud the most. So as we see cash return, fraud consists essentially of buying something with a false or stolen credit card number and then returning it in the real world for cash. And as we saw, the fraudsters especially take advantage of retailers that have weak policies in terms of returns or times of the year where those policies are weak just due to that time, for example, the holiday period.

Specific Executions: Collusive/ Affiliate Fraud

Let's talk about collusion and of heliotrope. These are two types of internal fraud, which are distinct, but similar causes of fraud. Means working with someone within an organization to bypass the fraud detection system or HUMINT. Fraud consists of using company money or stolen credit cards to gain affiliate commissions and fill your own pockets, which take a look at these two types. Internal frauds, as we mention, is any type of fraud that leverages inside knowledge of a company or retailer or bank by a first or a third party. We've been over this, but there are, however, two specific implementations of this. The first is collusive fraud. In this type of fraud, as the name says, a member of the organization colluded or cooperates with an external criminal such as a crime ring, and they share information with that fraudster, which then takes advantage of that information to bypass fraud detection rules.

Then a few troughs in this type of fraud the fraudster sets up. And if you were to count on some kind of platform, for example, for sales, then they use stolen credit card information to generate sales that provide them with affiliate commissions. Both types of internal froth are very hard to detect because they rely precisely on having knowledge of the internal fraud detection rules so that the perpetrator can avoid them. They are usually handled in the same way that dynamic fraud or morphing fraud is handled by staying flexible in the rules and the scores of the fraud monitoring system. Measures to fight this type of froth must include internal documentation, especially documentation of who has access to the fraud monitoring rules and their changes.

If only five people have access to fraud, monitoring rules in a type of criminal organization is able to bypass them easily. As you change the rules, make sure to document who knows about it, to associate that with whether the crime ring is able to bypass them or not. This way you can identify more. Other measures that can be used include velocity of use and change, as well as hot quests to catalog the known offenders, as well as possibly operational rules to flag repeaters fraud. What are some examples of collusive or if you get from the first example, is affiliate sales fraud. What we mention is a fraudster creates an account on an affiliate platform where it says, for example, you get 20% of every sale that is made with this referral code and then they use stolen credit cards to use that referral code and get affiliate commissions from this.

Another example is a retailer policy from when someone that belongs to the internal team of a retailer knows which chargebacks are automatically accepted. For example, every purchase for $10 and then sheets that information to consumer fraudsters who can ask for the money back on those transactions. It's another example of fraud. Monitoring fraud is the most dangerous time when the type of insider information that is leaked is actually fraud monitoring information, then the fraudster will have access to the exact rules that they can bypass, which can make them invisible and undetectable. What are our key takeaways here? The first is that internal fraud relies on insider knowledge to perform fraudulent transactions, in some cases by first parties, in some cases by third parties.

If fraud is a specific type of fraud, when someone internal colludes or collaborates with an external fraudster to leverage that inside information to bypass actual fraud detection and finally, a few IT fraud is a type of fraud where a fraudster sets up an affiliate account and pushes sales with stolen credit cards to obtain affiliate commissions, or, for example, where they use stolen credit cards to buy advertisements for real products and make a sale with them. So as we see, although the two types are distinct, they share the same principle. You are using company resources to either commit fraud or rent fraud. Go undetected and fill your own pockets.

Specific Executions: Dynamic/ Tested

Let's talk about the dynamic or test of froth, the most dangerous type of froth possible. This consists of testing the limits of rapid action and then changing your behavior to bypass them. For example, if every transaction a $500 jewelry is flagged, then they start to do 450. But when the limit is changed to 450, they shift to 400. It's a constant game of cat and mouse with the fraud detection system, and that's why it's so dangerous. Let's take a look that Emma Kraft, also known as morphing fraud, is the most dangerous type possible. The concept is very simple. It changes behavior based on what is detected. So instead of performing one type of fraud, an individual or more likely an organized crime ring will change their approach based on the feedback that is received.

You can almost think of it like a software tester, but instead of testing software to optimize it, the fraudster tests the fraud execution to optimize it. Instead, they find out what works. They double down on it and they get what isn't working. This type of fraud is a formidable challenge because no matter what changes or adjustments are made, the fraudster just keeps evolving with them. Dynamic froth can be detected using a couple of techniques, for example, using velocity of use and velocity of change to detect those changes. Using consumer identity checks or validating the delivery address, which is similar to other types of fraud, will usually be a drop off point.

But more than the actual techniques, it requires human intelligence to interpret.

If someone's purchases have been slowly changing nature in the past six months, an analyst is going to call that person. Maybe picking an experienced analyst that has experience with the nuances of these changes will be better than a newbie analyst. In some cases, the actual nature of the purchase will also help here. For example, having bought 20 chapter games over three months can be natural as a consumer, but having bought 25 screen TVs, well, maybe not so much. What are some examples of dynamic or testers from the first is having different accounts. This occurs when a crime ring uses a set of false accounts that make slow and steady purchases from different retailers over time.

Another variation that bursts out from this is when a crime ring uses multiple stolen cards, usually from vulnerable banks, and maxes out each one of them in a short amount of time or with different accounts in different purchases. And finally, another variation is having what could be called reasonable activity. Purchases are small and spread out over time, and they may change in nature, but they are the type of transaction that any person could reasonably make. What are our key takeaways here? The first is that the biggest danger of dynamic fraud is that it's tested just like a software product. The fraudsters figure out what works to test the fraud detection mechanisms in order to know how to avoid them. So they cut what doesn't work and they double down on what does work.

The biggest challenge of morphing fraud is that it keeps changing not once, not twice, but permanently. So the fraud monitoring system has to keep changing is the type of fraud that's in a kind of cat and mouse game. And finally, there are multiple subtypes of dynamic fraud, and you can fit in here as long as it changes by definition. So the purchase volumes, the number of accounts, the timelines all can change in many other elements as well. So as we see the dynamic or test of fraud is so dangerous because it keeps evolving in a constant game of cat and mouse with the fraud detection system. And you can think of it just like software testing, but instead of testing software to maximize its output, you're testing froth to maximize its efficiency. It's a perverse but very accurate metaphor.

Perpetrators: Intro

Let's talk about the perpetrators of fraud. Not all people who commit fraud have the same skill level or the same motivations. So it's important to cover the different types which can look at this group of topics that are not always committed by the same type of person. This is important to realize because different actors have different methodologies and motivations. Actors can range from casual to very skilled in technical terms, as well as having zero information about the actual fraud monitoring systems or complete information about them or anything in between. We can usually group fraud perpetrators into four major categories. In this chapter, we are going to cover those four major categories. The first are consumers. These are usually performed from on a very small scale, and they have no technological knowledge.

They just trick merchants into getting a free product or using it for free and returning it later. Then we have hackers and crackers. These are people with expert hacking skills, but they use them for different purposes. Hackers are usually ethical and they only want to show technical skill, while crackers usually have malicious intent. And then we have variations that suggest freaks, hacktivists and script kiddies. Then come white collar criminals. These are internal actors that leak information to ruin a company or to personally gain from the fraud. They can commit the fraud themselves or sell the information. And finally, we have organized crime, the most dangerous type. These are organized criminals that treat their fraud like a business to be optimized in cost, that we change tactics to optimize it. So as you see, we are going to cover the different perpetrators of fraud, which may have different skill levels and different motivations.

Perpetrators: Consumers

Talk about consumers. Consumers are probably the least dangerous type of fraudster because they can only commit fraud in the transactions that they are involved in. And unless these are of a high dollar value, they're not going to cause a lot of damage, but they can still cause damage. So let's take a look at them. Consumers are the most basic type of fraud perpetrator. They can't perform any type of fraud except for consumer shroff. Naturally, in the primitive to this type and the damage that it can cause, the type of fraud that they commit is usually only for personal gain, and it's generally very small in value. They only benefit from obtaining certain products for free or performing price arbitrage, from reselling a project at a higher price or using it and returning it in order to use it for free.

Consumers usually have one single motivation, which is personal gain on a small scale. They can be easily prevented by using basic measures such as a hotlist, which deters them after one or two attempts. But they can still cause some damage, especially if they perform fraud in terms of high value transactions. The most dangerous types of fraud related to retail or transactions are usually in large scale in their performance by multiple actors, usually organized criminals, and never by individual consumers. So these have very limited impact. What are some examples of fraud perpetrated by individual consumers? The first is satisfaction from consumers that keep returning items, claiming that they're not happy with them or others.

This is consumer satisfaction from another type is not that we are from consumers that claim to never receive the items dispatched despite the fact that all information points to the contrary in how we use in return is another variation. These are consumers that or their items in order to use them and then return the item claiming that there is a defect or other reasons. This is a type of fraud as well. What are our key takeaways here? The first is that consumers, as fraud perpetrators, have a very limited scope. They cause very little damage. They can only dispute the transactions related to them and with limited effect, they can be easily stopped. Since they are one individual in usually using their own account information, they can easily be stopped with a hotlist which prevents them from returning items or requesting refunds over and over.

They have one or two opportunities. There are fine lines with consumers. Although fraud is possible infrequently. In some cases the usage is valid. So it's important to distinguish between both. For example, it is possible that someone did not receive four items in a row. It's not likely, but it is possible. So as we see, consumers are generally the least dangerous type of fraudster because they commit fraud in large quantities and they can easily be stopped. But it's important to notice when an item that was not returned or an item that was counterfeit was a real situation versus fraud.

Perpetrators: Hackers and Crackers

Let's talk about headers and crackers. These are usually fraudsters who use their I.T. expertise in order to commit fraud. However, there are different types and hackers are not even the worst type. So let's take a look. One of the types of perpetrators of fraud are both hackers and crackers. While they are similar in their technical skills. They have different motivations. So it's important to distinguish between them. So hackers usually have the goal of exploiting vulnerabilities just to show technical prowess, to show that they can do it. As the name says, they love to hack processes and find shortcuts. They are usually ethical in nature and they break into systems in private to then reveal their exploits to the organization itself.

They don't have malicious intent in most cases. They do it just to show that they can. Crackers, however, are the malicious version of hackers. These are hackers that break into systems for personal gain or to resell the information. There are also different variations of crackers. One variation on freaks, which are crackers specializing in phone hacking, for example, using sounds with specific frequencies to bypass authorization of phone systems and perform authorized operations. Script kiddies are a variation of crackers that don't have hacking skills personally, and they usually use ready to use tools. They're usually in the form of scripts.

Therefore, the name, they usually also have malicious intent, but they cause limited damage because the only thing that they can do is render scripts if anything is needed. Besides that, they immediately run into a wall. While hackers themselves don't usually exploit vulnerabilities for personal use in the usually warn organizations so that they can improve. Crackers have the exact same skills, but they have malicious intent and they want to have a trough for personal use. When this happens, it's usually still on a small scale and only for personal enrichment. So while a crime ring may still use hundreds of credit card numbers in a process based on that, an individual cracker may steal two or three credit card numbers by themselves from a TV in a PlayStation, for example.

So they are dangerous, but compared to crime rings in very limited scope, unless, Of course, they manage to pull out a major hack and pull off a leak, such as, for example, the Panama Papers or the Equifax Weak Bay in general, they have limited scope. There is a subtype of hackers, however, that can cause damage. Who are known as hacktivists, as the portmanteau says. They are a mix of both hackers and activists. So these are hackers that still don't want to personally gain from a situation, but they may leverage the fraud to aid a specific political cause. For example, activists that are against weapons manufacturers may aid fraud of a specific weapons manufacturer database to bankrupt them and compromise their operational chain with the goal of decreasing arms sales volumes, or to compromise an oil company to save the environment or similar depending on the cause.

What are some examples of hackers and crackers? The first are ethical hackers, as the name says. These are people that just want to hack systems and find out vulnerabilities for the pleasure of showing technical prowess. And they usually warned the institution in private. The second type are penetration testers. These are hackers that are professionally hired by an institution to figure out what their vulnerabilities are and demonstrate exploiting them so that they can be fixed. They are hired to be hackers, in a way. And finally, script kiddies. These usually use premade and ready to use tools possibly sold by a cracker that productize their hacking skills. These tools usually only do one thing and exploit only one issue. So the script kitty runs the tool to find vulnerable systems, and when this one doesn't work, they can't do anything else.

What are our key takeaways here? The first is that different hackers in crackers have different intentions. Hackers are usually ethical and are focused on their achievements. While crackers are the opposite. They're focused on personal enrichment. But both have subtypes. Hacktivists are a specific type of hacker that still doesn't want to personally gain, but they want someone to personally lose by defending the specific political cause. And finally, script kiddies are crackers. They don't hack by themselves, but they use pre-made tools. These have limited scope and cause limited damage. So as you see, there are multiple types of fraudsters with a high level of I.T. skills. In hackers, usually you just want to demonstrate expertise and are not coalitions. The malicious ones are the crackers.

Perpetrators: White-Collar Criminals

Let's talk about white collared actors. These are people within the company that commit fraud being employees of it, or at least facilitated for it. But they can have different motivations. So let's take a look at them. White collar actors or white collar criminals are actors with inside information within a company or institution that helped bring down the company or cause damage to it, either by themselves or by facilitating fraud by a third party. So every time that we are talking about internal fraud or collusive fraud, it's usually caused by white collar criminals and the company itself. While their motivations can be varied, they usually have a vested interest in the products committed. They either want to leverage it for personal career progression or even blackmail their superiors, or they just want to actively damage the company or specific people within it.

They may want to improve themselves or damage the company. Sometimes both internal actors can be very dangerous in the more information that they possess in terms of fraud detection or internal security mechanisms. The more dangerous they are. It's almost like those spy movies where you have a mole. The higher up the mole is, the more damage they can cause because the more sensitive information they know. The epitome of this is having white collar criminals within the fraud monitoring department itself. This is the nightmare scenario. They will have access to all information about actual fraud prevention.

So selling this information to hackers or criminal gangs can be completely devastating to a company because the fraud perpetrators can avoid all security checks, institution flags, jewelry transactions starting at 4 p.m. for new accounts above $1,000 in a criminal ring that knows about that rule. Or just do a transaction for $9.99 and so on. Of course, if you're using fraud scoring in artificial intelligence, it's not that clear. But you do see my point. The impact of white collar criminals on an organization can be moderate to very severe. In this, the patterns depend both on the type of internal information that they have, whether it's generic or whether it's specific security information and also who they sell it to.

What are some examples of white collar actors? One is, how are the exploits of an internal employee that is fired by a retailer before the holiday season and that has information about their dispute procedures so information on how those disputes are resolved to a crime ring which can then exploit it during this holiday period, which is the most sensitive time for it. Another example is taking the CEO down and this satisfied the executive may want to take their CEO down by selling vulnerability information to crime rings which can exploit it and then leak information that the CEO knew about the vulnerability to compromise them. And finally, an insider with information on consumer transaction policies can leverage this information to make fraudulent purchases themselves.

Profiting from this. What are our key takeaways here? The first is that insiders can be first or third party. White power actors usually use information to cause the company harm either by doing it themselves, which is first party, or by selling the information to someone else, which is third party. They usually use this information to cause the company harm, either to personally gain or at least to make the company lose. Sometimes both. They may have differing motivations. They can be motivated by personal greed to rise in the corporation or by revenge, deciding to take the company down again. In some very worst cases, it can be both. They may want the company to suffer so that the current people are fired and they can be promoted.

The damage that they cause can be moderate to very severe. It depends on what type of information they have access to and who they convey to or sell it to. You can easily see the difference between having information on returns for a local retailer branch and giving it to a single cracker, versus having information on worldwide return policies and giving that to an organized crime ring. So as we see, white collar actors can facilitate fraud in the first or the third person, and the damage that it can cause can be moderate to severe, depending on the sensitivity of the information that they use to commit fraud.

Perpetrators: Organized Crime Rings

Let's talk about organized crime. These are definitely the most dangerous type of fraudster because they have a lot of resources and they can use the most advanced types of fraud, such as dynamic or tested from at the end of the day. They treat the fraud like a business that they must optimize to maximize their revenue. Let's take a look. Organized crime rings are usually the most dangerous type of fraud perpetrator that exists. Their motivations go beyond personal gain and usually revolve around the systematic enrichment of their organization and members. They are so dangerous because they literally treat their crime like a business where they must put their employees to work and make as much profit as possible.

Crime rings are the most likely type of perpetrator to use dynamic or morphing fraud because they are the ones that truly have the resources to test the vulnerabilities of different websites or corporations. And the patience to learn from them and to keep trying. They can also, in many cases, include other types of perpetrators as accomplices or employees such as white collar criminals to obtain inside information or crackers to perform an explicit exploit. The element that makes organized crime so dangerous is precisely in their name, as we stated. They are organized and efficient. They treat their crime like a business where they continuously test new products and strategies to improve their margins and make use of their current workforce.

Not only do organized crime rings spend a lot of time and effort figuring out the different vulnerabilities in exploiting them, but they spend an equal amount of time hiding their activity. This creates a twin challenge of both identifying the fraud committed by them and then stopping it. What are some examples of organized crime? The first is organized identity theft. An organized crime ring may have multiple people allocated to car rental hotels or other establishments as fake staff to swipe real world information, or even using methods such as phishing or going for trash so that they can then impersonate these people.

Organized crime can also buy what are called data dumps. When independent crackers obtain information from corporations, they can sell it online for profit or even make other criminals before it on auctions, on the dark web, for example. So crime rings can obtain this information and then use it, for example, to make bust out purchases with or gather credit cards. Organized crime rings can leverage insiders in companies to avoid the fraud detection rules of given companies in order to steer clear of detection. What are our key takeaways here? The first is that organized is the key word in organized crime. They are so dangerous because, as the name says, they are organized. They treat their illegal operations as a business that must be optimized in terms of profit and margins.

There are different actors that may be included by them. They can bring crackers along for a specific operation or white collar criminals to obtain information on a specific company. They use them as a kind of contractor for crime. Although crime rings vary in strategy. The dangerous thing about it is that they keep optimizing these strategies, which is a big headache for fraud managers, because any additional safeguard that an institution provides will be bypassed in a matter of time. Both have to keep evolving. So as we see, organized crime rings are in the business of crime. They employ different actors for specific purposes and they optimize the work that needs to be done to maximize their revenue. They usually have a lot of resources and they use the most sophisticated types of fraud.

Recap

We are now at the end of the Fraud Approaches chapter. Let's take a moment just to recap the different topics that we've covered, the strategies, executions, the actors, as well as consolidate our knowledge with some questions. We are now at the end of the Fraud Approaches chapter where we covered the different strategies and executions of frogs by different actors. In this chapter, we covered three major topics in terms of how Frog is actually performed. First, we covered the general strategies in terms of obtaining and using information social engineering, identity theft and others. Then we covered specific execution types. Cash return from card, black frog, dynamic front and others.

And finally, we covered the different perpetrator types, including hackers and crackers, criminals and others. Some questions that you can ask yourself to consolidate the knowledge in this chapter include What is the difference between social engineering and identity theft? Which one is more dangerous? What is the difference between a hacker and a cracker? How do the motivations of these two differ among themselves, and how do they differ from the motivation of a crime ring? For example, what is the difference between consumer fraud in general and cash return from I.D.

done by the same actors? What is the biggest parallel of dynamic and morphing fraud? What is the time of the year that is the most sensitive for cash return from? And what is the most dangerous type of internal information that internal actors or white collar criminals can share? I would also ask who is the most dangerous type of perpetrator that they can share it with? We close the Fraud Approaches chapter where we try to cover who this fraud and how they do it.

Fraud Prevention Techniques Intro

We are now at the Fraud Prevention Techniques chapter, which is going to be the bulk of this Book. In this chapter, we are going to cover almost every single type of fraud technique imaginable, from fraud scoring to identity verification, address verification, physical devices, and a lot more. Let's take a moment to cover the topics and goals for this chapter. Welcome to the Fraud Prevention Techniques chapter, where we are going to cover specific techniques of different categories that can be used for fraud prevention. In terms of progress, we are now at this second chapter three.

In the first chapter, we cover the different approaches: who are the perpetrators? What are their general strategies in terms of acquiring and using information and the specific executions of from? In the second chapter, we are going to cover the different fraud prevention techniques, how to verify identities, and data in other checks that can be made to detect and prevent fraud. And in the fraud chapter, we are going to cover the fraud monitoring strategy itself, how to select the tools to create a bigger strategy, what guidelines to follow in terms of data usage and processing, among other considerations. What is our major goal for this chapter? Well, it's to cover the different fraud prevention techniques that can be leveraged by different systems in higher detail.

We are going to cover, for example, the different types of verification that can be performed on the consumers account information both automatically and manually. How certain processes like insurance and guarantees can help prevent fraud but can add certain costs. How fraud scoring in rules engines can be used together to score fraud. How technology can be leveraged to authenticate specific devices or even place the consumer in a specific location at a specific time. Or how to average automatic lookups and checks of account information such as addresses and phone numbers.

To achieve this, we are going to cover five key categories of techniques that can be used for fraud prevention. The first is data verification, verifying specific data elements associated with a consumer to decrease front risk. The second category is identity verification techniques to identify the actual consumer of a transaction in their identity. The first is technological verification leveraging technology such as electronic signatures or device authentication to help identify the consumer in a transaction. Fourth, come front scoring and rules.

Two approaches to fraud monitoring that some people may think are competing but can actually be used in combination in finally come processes, actual services provided by banks or insurance companies that can be used to help decrease fraud risk for merchants. So as you see in this chapter, we are going to cover all the types possible of fraud prevention techniques.

Data Verification: Intro

Let's convert data verification techniques. As the name indicates, these are techniques that verifies specific data points to indicate where the fraud is occurring or not. The bank account, the credit card and more. Let's take a look. Besides verifying the person's identity. There are other elements of the transaction that can be verified as well. With the goal of trying to identify the probability of fraud in a given transaction, this includes leveraging techniques such as velocity checks, which verify how frequently an information element is used or changed, as well as the verification of transaction information such as the consumer's credit card or bank account.

In order to achieve this. We are going to cover three key types of verifications in terms of data related to the transaction. The first are velocity checks, in short, verifying both how frequently something is used or how frequently it changes. For example, verifying how frequently a given credit card was used in a specific time period, or how frequently the rest of the account information changes associated with that card. Then actual card verifications, verifying both the card number with a couple of checks which provide information related to the issuer, bank and others, but also using card security schemes such as CV to make sure that the consumer really has access to the card. And finally, will cover.

Charge and deposits. Verifications. Charge. Verification consists of calling the bank to verify a transaction, while deposit verifications consist of making a deposit in the consumer's bank account to verify that account. Both take more time, but provide an added layer of authentication. So as we see in this group of topics, we're going to cover techniques that verify data related to the transaction.

Data Verification: Velocity Checks

Let's talk about velocity checks. Velocity checks are a staple of many fraud prevention solutions. In essence, says they indicate the frequency with which a piece of information is used or changed. For example, if your credit card is used 50 times in a day, that's a high velocity of use. Or if for the same account, a person tries to use 50 different credit cards. That's a high velocity of change. Let's take a look at how these work velocity checks. As the name says, verify the speed at which specific information is used or changed. For example, the number of times that any specific credit card has been used in a period of time or the number of times that the address associated with it has been changed in that period of time.

There are two main categories of velocity checks that are frequently used. The first or velocity of use checks. This metric captures the number of times that a certain information fuel has been used in a given amount of time. For example, the number of times that a given credit card has been used within six months, for example, or the number of times the same phone number hasn't been used in that period of time. The same shipping address. And so on. Then we have velocity of change checks. These work in a similar manner, but they capture the number of times that an information field has been changed in that given amount of time. For example, it can detect the number of times that a card number has changed associated with this same shipping address within six months.

While each of these checks can be used to detect obvious types of fraud. For example, the velocity of use checks can easily detect by start activity where countless purchases are made with the same card. In velocity of change, checks can be used to detect card fraud, where multiple card numbers will be used with the same shipping address or number. In reality, they are more efficient in combination with other measures. They are considered almost a staple of any fraud monitoring solution, and they work especially well combined with other measures such as hard wastes, identity verification, front scoring models and others.

What are some examples of velocity checks? Velocity of use, for example, can be used to detect how frequently a credit card is used, but also other fields. For example, it can detect the usage of the same fake shipping address for multiple purchases. Velocity of change checks can be used to detect dynamic or morphing fraud or just fraud at scale because the same card numbers will be used with different names and different addresses. And finally, these all-city checks can be used in both single merchant or multiple merchant variations.

They can take into account just the consumers of one merchant or multiple. And naturally, any system that does the latter was attacked by fraudulent usage or changing information much more easily because they have more data. What are our key takeaways here? The first is that velocity views the text, the speed at which an information element such as a credit card number is used within a given time period. The second is velocity of change. This is the text, the speed at which an information element such as an address is changed within a given time period.

And finally, velocity checks are usually used as part of big solutions. They are powerful on their own, but they become even more powerful when combined with other tools and with data from multiple merchants. So as we see, velocity of checks can be applied to the use of a piece of information or the changes of that piece of information. And they are usually staples of any fraud prevention solution together with other techniques.

Data Verification: Card Verification

Let's talk about cards, verifications. These are verifications that check whether the card number is valid or not. And then in some cases, even assess the level of risk in a transaction. Let's take a look at how these work. Verifying that the credit card which was used is valid is very important. There are a few techniques included in this group with different levels of complexity. The first is the loan verification or month ten verification. It's a simple check and formula. It validates that the credit card being used is in fact valid. It's usually performed before even sending the credit card number to the bank.

Then we have the PIN verification or bank identification number verification. This check is similar to the above, but it goes beyond it. It takes the first six digits of the card, which are unique, and can identify the card's bank issuer and other information such as the card tier, for example. And finally, we have an additional security layer in the form of card security schemes, CV, CV two and others. These are an additional verification that is useful for transactions where the card is not present. They consist of making the consumer enter the three digits on the back of the card. Besides the card number, these decrease the chances of a fraudster using a stolen credit card number because if they only have the number, they won't have the CV.

While the DNA verification in math ten verifications are more about data integrity. In other words, making sure that the incorrect information is not sent to the bank, which wastes time and money for everyone involved. They are actually also good to detect card fraud because a lot of unsuccessful attempts that don't pass these checks or a lot of invalid card numbers may mean that someone is a brute forcing a large quantity of card numbers where the card like attack the CV or CV to check in particular is useful to make sure that the card holder really is in possession of the card. Because without this check, anyone that swipes the full card number can just use the card without any consequence.

And that is why most retailers nowadays use CV or CV too, but some still don't. What are some examples of card verification? The first is Martin, which acts as a checksum. The Mark ten verification, also known as the one verification or one algorithm, is a checksum algorithm. In short, it makes sure that the card number obeys a certain set of rules and that it's valid that the integrity of that number was not compromised. TV and CBT two are widely implemented nowadays, especially as a measure against scammers. It doesn't matter how many full card numbers you can swipe. As long as you don't have the CV number in. Finally, the PIN number is an example of a block of very specific information.

These first six digits tell you a lot of information, including the issuer of the card, the level of the card, whether it's platinum premium or others, and even the country of the issuer. What are our key takeaways here? The MOF ten or one algorithm is a checksum technique. It makes sure that the card is valid. It's also used to help flag multiple incorrect numbers, such as four card walks from the bin or bank identification number. Consists of the first six digits of the number and it contains a lot of information about the card issuer, the bank, the card level and more. It's used to not just verify the number, but also to evaluate the transaction risk of that card.

The CPV and CTD two numbers, among others, also known collectively as card security schemes, consist of the three digits on the back of the card that must be entered. It's an additional layer of protection. So as we see techniques like the one algorithm or the VIN number help verify that the credit card number really is real. But in some cases, the CV, for example, takes it one step further and actually verifies that this person really owns the card.

Data Verification: Charge/Deposit Verifications

Let's talk about charge and deposit verifications. These are two different techniques, which are a little bit more advanced in consumer resources, but also provide a higher level of protection. So charge verification is about calling the bank to verify a transaction, while deposit verifications are about verifying a bank account by making a deposit in that account. Let's take a look. These two techniques can provide an additional level of security, although they take time and there are costs involved. The first is charge verification. This consists of the merchant calling the bank or the card issuer and actually verifying the transaction.

The charge, as you may be guessing. This is costly and it relies on the bank having staff on hand just to answer these calls. This is a service that usually is reserved for high value borrowers because otherwise it doesn't make sense. Another type is deposit verification. This is a technique where the retailer or the platform makes a small deposit in the consumer's bank account and asks them to verify it. It's used to make sure that the consumer really has access to the bank account that they're using. It does take time and it doesn't stop many cases of identity theft where the fraudster also has access to the victim's bank account.

But it does stop a lot of other types of fraud. What are some examples of charge and deposit verifications? The first is PayPal, an example of a platform that uses deposit verification.

When you register, they make a small transfer to a bank account and you must confirm it before you start using the platform. The second is Bitcoin brokers, where now that I think about it, any kind of broker as well. These used deposit checks due to the amount of anonymous fraud that's going on making trades with other people's money. So the same mechanism. You have to verify a small deposit made to your bank account to verify that account, and then you can start trading in finally high value transactions.

This is a type of transaction where charge verification is common. For example, if a celebrity makes a 250 K transfer to pay for a car in one go, my guess is that the merchant is going to use charge verification for that one. What are our key takeaways here? The first is charge verification. It consists of the merchant calling the bank and verifying the actual transaction information with the bank itself. And usually it's a member of the bank staff doing it manually. The second is deposit verification. Deposit checks consist of the merchant depositing a small quantity in the consumer's account and having them verify it in order to verify that actual bank account use.

And finally, both of these involve more time and more money. These additional verifications should be saved for transactions that actually offset these costs, not the low value ones. So as we see, these are two different but related techniques for providing an additional layer of information before authorizing a transaction. And although they consume more resources and more time, they provide an additional layer of security for that transaction.

Identity Verification: Intro

Let's discover identity verification. As the name says in this group of techniques, we are going to cover how to verify specific parts of the person's identity, their address, their presence in a blacklist and so on. Let's take a look at this group of topics. Verifying the consumer's identity is naturally extremely important in terms of monitoring fraud, and there are multiple techniques that can be used to perform this with different levels of effort and time consumption involved. We are going to cover techniques that can both identify a consumer themselves, but also key pieces of their information, such as their address or others through a myriad of means in terms of identity verification.

We are going to cover five key types of techniques that can be of use. The first are wastes both negative lists that contain records of consumers, but also positive lists which contain trusted consumers. Then, simple field verifications, verifying fields such as the consumer's age, email or telephone number. After that address, verifications verifying both the mailing address of the person, which is fast and it's usually included in credit card checks themselves, but also possibly the shipping address, which has more effort involved but provides an extra layer of security.

After this will cover menu authentication, both manual information obtained by banks to confirm consumer information as part of Know Your Customer Regulations, but also our wallet checks, which consist of calling the consumer and asking about details of their past transaction history to confirm their identity. And finally, automated lookups, quick lookups of the consumer's phone and address for confirmation purposes. So as we see in this group of topics, we are going to cover techniques that verify parts of the person's identity.

Identity Verification: Lists

Let's talk about lists. Lists are a staple of any fraud prevention solution. There are multiple types, but the most common type are hot lists. That is, lists of known offenders who are not allowed to use their credit card again or their email or other types of information. But there are also other types of lists for other purposes. Let's take a look. Keeping lists of both positive and negative consumers to keep track of their behavior is especially important to prevent consumers from. Common types of lists include. First, what are known as hard lists or blacklists.

These are lists of consumers to block the usually fake consumers that have already committed fraud in the past. And they are blocked. They are consulted before a transaction to block the transaction before it even occurs. They can be hot lists of credit cards, shipping addresses, or other information. Warm lists are kind of the intermediate step. They are lists of consumers that are, quote unquote, risky. They may have not committed fraud precisely, but they have partaken in questionable practices such as returns due to not being satisfied, which kind of puts them at risk. They are borderline fraudsters in a way.

Usually this is the stepping stone to a hard list, as we're going to see later. And finally, we have white lists or positive lists. These are lists of consumers that show positive behavior and they're trusted. For example, if you have an extravagant consumer, it makes very high purchases from different points in the world.

And you're used to it. You can put them on a white list so that their behavior is not flagged as fraud. Hubris or blacklists are the most common type. These can be created based on multiple elements of the accounts information. So there may be a hotlist for credit cards.

There may be a hotlist for phone numbers and so on. And it's common for there to be cross checks in a way. If a credit card gets flagged, then the shipping address for that card may be flagged as well in another hotlist. Here's the thing. These are not going to help a lot against one time fraud or dynamic form as you're probably thinking. But they can be very effective against most other methods if they're using a block attack with multiple credit card numbers. But one single shipping address, just hotlist that address and they're dead in the water.

Or are they using the same credit card to make multiple orders at a retailer for cash? Returns hard with that credit card and there's not something that's similar to these lists or what are called the ninth party checks. These are checks on public databases. It depends on the country of parties that are denied from doing business due to suspicions of fraud. They are public lists, in a way. And if your country allows for them, they should also be leveraged. What are some examples of lists that first are blacklists of credit cards? These are essential to keep track of the fraudulent card numbers used across retailers and can stop offenders. Going from warm to hot is another example for some retailers.

A good strategy can be to place one problematic customer on a warm place and then upgrade them to a hot list. If they make another mistake. This way they get the benefit of the doubt once or twice before their flag. If someone who commits fraud in finally listing someone's phone or address besides the credit card is another example. And it's useful especially for card walk attacks, because each card number is different, but different cards may have the same phone or address associated with them. What are our key takeaways here? The first is that hot lists or blacklists are used to keep track of fraudsters. These can be lists for credit card information or other elements such as phones or addresses. Usually there's a list for each. Then we have warm lists in some cases.

Warm lists are used as an intermediate step. They allow for one offense before the person is placed on an actual hotlist. And finally, positive wastes are used in some cases. They contain trusted consumers that show exemplary behavior, and they are used to make sure that random behavior by these people is not considered thorough. So as we see, lists are a staple of many fraud prevention solutions. Pathways are the most common type where people are actually. BLOCK Then you have warm lists, which is kind of the intermediate step to a hotlist. And in some cases, you also have wait lists for trusted individuals.

Identity Verification: Simple Field Verification

Let's talk about simple field verifications. These are verifications of, as the name says, simple fields like email, phone number or age. And these are not very sophisticated. And they don't stop all types of fraud, but they do stop the less sophisticated types where the person doesn't even have an email or phone number. Let's take a look. There is a set of quick and simple checks that can be performed to validate elements of a person's identity through their account information. Usually these are not very deep at all and only provide a basic level of authentication. In many cases, they're the starting point. The first type is age verification.

This is simply making the consumer verify their age. In some cases, they may just have to enter it at the start of a website, for example, or by providing a document. Naturally, these two different variations have different levels of authentication, but also different impacts on transactions. Making a person upload a document can make a lot of people cancel their order. But in some industries, like the adult one or the alcohol one or gambling, they may be required. The second type is email verification. This is just making the consumer verify their email account. It may be with a permanent link or with a temporary link.

So if you've ever registered for a website and they say, just confirm your email, this is this especially for certain industries such as financial services. Besides the person verifying their email the first time. They may also have to verify the email on every single transaction, usually with the use of a one time password or a code. This is additional security, but it may delay or even cancel themselves. A third type is DNI or telephone number identification. This is a bit more advanced. It's a system that, based on a phone number, determines the type of phone that is being used and even where it came from. The price may vary based on the country, but it's relatively inexpensive.

These verifications usually validate specific fields of the cardholder's account. Data in the are the first layer of authentication before more complex techniques are used afterwards. So while these provide almost no protection in terms of high risk and high value transactions, they can be useful to use in mass for low value transactions because they immediately eliminate a portion of unsophisticated fraudsters that didn't properly obtain an email or phone. So, for example, if someone is buying a car, making them verify, the email is not going to do a lot. You need more sophisticated techniques.

But if you have 10,000 people buying products, making them verify their email may already slice a portion of those transactions. That may be fraud because the person doesn't even have an email. An important note is that address verifications, especially for the shipping address, also count as these but those merit discussing on their own because there are multiple methods to do it. As with anything, these additional verifications may cause a drop in good orders because every additional roadblock, like an email confirmation, makes some people drop their order. But in some cases they are actually necessary.

For example, for certain industries like alcohol, gambling and others, age verification is necessary and in financial services. Usually all of these verifications and even more are required. What are some examples of simple field verifications? The first is saying age is necessary. Some specific industries, such as gambling, alcohol or the products actually require age verification before any purchase is even made. The second example is OTP is one time passwords. In some cases, OTP is sent to the person's email or phone to validate a transaction. Especially in home banking interfaces. It slows down the process, but it's more protection.

And finally, we have phone verification. It can be interesting to detect severe discrepancies such as a consumer in the U.S. that tends to ration phone number or the opposite. What are our key takeaways here? The first is age verification. This is merely the verification of the consumer's age, which is usually done with a document. The second type is email verification. This is simply by verifying the person's email address before the purchase form. It can be done just when the account is created or on. Every transaction. And finally, we have TNI telephone number verification.

This technique allows a merchant to verify the phone number of the consumer and find out more about their location, among other details which can reveal interesting or dangerous information. So as we see, these simple few verifications are not going to prevent most types of fraud. However, they can prevent the less sophisticated types where the person doesn't even have an ID, phone number or others.

Identity Verification: Address Verifications

Let's talk about address verifications. Verifying the address of a person is an important step to prevent fraud. Usually there are many services even included in the credit card companies themselves which verify the billing address. But we can take it one step further and even verify the actual shipping address. Let's take a look at these and more. There are three types of verifications that can be performed on the consumer's address, billing or shipping. These are good to prevent fraud based on false shipping locations such as dropoff points. The first is alias or Address Verification Services. These verify the billing address associated with the cardholder's card. It's easy to check if the billing information is entered into the website or not. Some cards support a fee, which is advanced address verification.

These verify not just the billing address, but the shipping address and contact information as well. But only some card associations support it. Then we have delivery address verification. This is a technique that consists of a service that checks the shipping address of the consumer to make sure it's valid and that it's not a drop off point or another type of false address that is not a real home or office. Naturally, this is more costly, but it's also more helpful to prevent fraud that relies on drop off points or invalid shipping addresses. And finally, freight forwarding your verification. This technique checks whether this address is a freight forwarder or not.

Or, in other words, if it's an address that automatically routes, packages and shipments to another address, possibly an international one. This is going to prevent international forwarding fraud, which is when someone or there's a project that is going to be shipped to an address. It seems to be in the same country, but that address automatically reroutes it internationally, while verification of the billing address is cheap and widely accessible. EVs, for example, are available for most cards in a V for some of them, and are actually usually part of the bigger card's verification process. So it's very natural.

The verification of the shipping address, on the other hand, is more costly, but it's justifiable for high value transactions. It's particularly useful to stop all types of fraud that rely on false shipping addresses, such as cash returned from one time fraud in others. All of these use drop off points or other fake addresses so that the perpetrator can pick up the package quickly and then either return it or fence it. These verifications prevent those fake addresses from being used. Which one of these to use depends on the combination of other techniques present and the type of fraud there is to our suspicion. What are some examples of address verification? The first is freight forwarding, as we mentioned.

Checking for freight forwarding is a great tool to prevent international travel with a shipping location, for example, maybe in the U.S. but the package ends up internationally. If you don't check for freight forwarding, you'll never know that. The second example is Alias address. Verification for the billing address is completely standard, and it's usually included in the most basic types of card verification services provided by associations. And it can be good to solve disputes. There are different levels and matches. Each of these techniques returns a result.

What is called a signal in the fraud monitoring terminology or one in programming language is called a return of a function, and it usually is not a yes no, but it's a full match in case the address is a full match, a partial match and not available, and so on. So the fraud monitoring systems must take into account these different levels of responses. What are our key takeaways here? The first is ABS Asia, and these are two types of dealing address verification, both included in basic cards verification services. ISVs is more widespread, while a V is just for specific cards. Delivery address verification, as the name says, verifies the shipping address.

It's more costly, but it's especially important to prevent fraud that relies on drop off points and invalid addresses. And finally, freight forwarder verification, especially important to prevent international travel, because, you know, beforehand, whether this address is a freight forwarder that is going to forward this problem. From a domestic address to an international one waiter. So as we see, there are multiple services that allow you to verify a person's address. Verifying the billing address takes less time, but provides less protection. Verifying the shipping address or even checking for freight forwarders takes more resources and more time, but provides an extra layer of security.

Identity Verification: Manual Authentication

Let's talk about menu authentication. There are two main types, but it consists of manually verifying the person's identity as your guest. This takes a lot more time and resources than other techniques because you actually need resources, manpower to actually get this done. But it provides an extra layer of security that many other techniques just don't provide. Let's take a look. There are two types of techniques that rely on manually confirming the person's identity, either internally or through direct contact with them. These are respectively the first manual identity authentication. This consists of an internal analyst searching for public information that can corroborate someone's identity.

It's usually done on the bank level and not merchant level. So if someone just opened an account as John Smith leaving on Maple Avenue. One, two, three. An analyst is going to search for this name and this address on the Internet and specifically on the lookup engines, and they will gauge how much they can find on the person. It can be as simple as finding their name, location and date of birth online in a public database to make sure that they are a real person. It's also a known customer requirement for many banks. The other methods are out of wallet checks, also known as out of pocket checks.

These consist of calling a consumer and asking them questions about nonpublic parts, transactions or credit from their account, or, in other words, information that they don't have in their pocket. You can consider this the equivalent of the security questions when you lose your password. But these are specifically about the account transactions. These are great defined chargebacks because they can easily identify imposters that don't have access to the person's bank account and just the card. It stops most identity theft as well. But it does not stop identity theft that is so severe that the fraudster has to have access to the person's account for years.

These are two examples of techniques that do take time, and they're more costly, mainly because they involve human capital, which immediately makes the process manual and not automatic. But they can be effective for high value or high risk transactions that do merit them. They are great in particular to dispute chargebacks where the cardholder information doesn't match the real one so they can easily stop fraudsters from impersonating someone. If you are using a card block attack and you use a false name and address in a false phone, you may both be stopped by the fact that the bank of that merchant will find no public information on you, but also by the fact that if they call you, you are going to know nothing about the bank accounts history.

In some cases, a technique called phone verification is used. It simply consists of calling the consumer and verifying a transaction to make sure that they're really doing it. You can almost consider this an out of wallet check, but without the questions, just a call. It's important to notice this is not a silver bullet. However, there are severe cases of identity theft where the fraudster has had control of the account for so long and including the bank account that they can pass out of wallet checks. But these are not very frequent. What are some examples of manual authentication? The first is a call from the bank. If you've ever tried to buy something and the bank called you, that was a phone verification.

If they ask you some questions as well, that was an out of wallet check. The second is to know your customer requirements. Manual authentication of the consumer by searching public information is an actual requirement to know your customer regulation. For a lot of banks. The customer's identity must be verified with data. In cases where no information is gathered on the client, a bank may actually refuse to open an account for them. And finally pass transaction data. This is what out of wallet checks focus on. They are about past credit or transactions and they can identify a lot of fraudsters that don't have the answers.

What are our key takeaways with identity verification? The first is manual authentication. It's the process of manually searching for information that backs up a person's identity on the Internet, and it's usually done by banks as part of Know Your Customer Regulations, both when they open an account, but also periodically after that. The second method is out of wallet checks. These are verifications. Then, by calling a person and asking them a specific question. And only the account holder with no. It catches all fraudsters that don't have account taxes. And finally, both of these take time and money.

These techniques are some of the most reliable, but also some of the most costly because they cannot be automated and they rely on actual people. So as we see whether you are actively searching for information on the person or calling them to check those details, you don't take more time and resources, but provide an extra layer of security that you only get by speaking with the person.

Identity Verification: Automated Lookups

Let's talk about automated lookups that are taking a person's phone or email address and doing a reverse search to see if that information matches what you have on file. This is usually not active. We use fraud prevention techniques. Just a backup to corroborate the information which you already have. Let's take a look at how it works. There are three techniques that relied on automatically looking up information on the cardholder to obtain support information about the validity of a transaction. These automated lookups confirm components of the cardholder's account information, so they are many times. The first is phone workups. This is an automated service that is used to verify the cardholder's phone number.

The second are address lookups. They are similar, but they are for the person's address instead of phone number. If you yourself ever tried to look up an address online and then got the person associated with that address, you've used one of these services. It's important to note that they can be faulty in some cases, such as for families that move a lot, such as military families. And they can also fail in specific around someone's time of moving because the platform has not been updated yet. And finally, we have credit lookups. These are more expensive than the other two, but they are very complete.

They provide full information about the person, including their address, their phone, their ID and more. All of these mechanisms are not usually used as stand alone techniques, but instead are automatic contingencies to verify information that has already been entered or obtained. They are a double check, if you will, on the information that you already have. While cell phone and address lookups are simple and cheap, they can fail due to inconsistently answered information or, as we saw, rapidly changing information that has just not been propagated yet. Private lookups, however, on their own, are more expensive than the other types, and they provide a lot more information. But they are not foolproof.

In some cases, agencies can make mistakes in entering the information so they can fail as well, albeit less often than the other two types. What are some examples of automated lookups? The first is the WACC period. As we saw, both phone and address lookups may fail not just due to incorrect information, but also due to periods because changes can take weeks or even months to be propagated. These solutions can be combined. These lookups can be combined with other techniques such as velocity checks, card number checks lists. Or they can just serve as double checks for information that was already entered by the consumer. And finally, especially for credit checks, their usage must be justified. Since credit lookups are so costly, they should only be used for the transactions that do offset the cost.

What are our key takeaways here? The first are phone lookups. They consist of looking at someone's phone number to obtain information about it. The second are address lookups. Same, but for the person's address. They can be faulty in case the person most frequently has changed recently, or if the information is just entered wrongly. And finally, credit lookups are similar to the other two types, but they are more expensive. They are also a lot more complete, providing a 360 degree view on the consumer's information. So as you see, we can do workouts of simple information like phone numbers or addresses where more complex ones like credit scores. But at the end of the day, these are just a backup to gauge whether the information they already have matches it or not.

Technological Verification: Intro

Let's talk about technological verification techniques. These techniques use some sort of technology from the GPS location to cookies, smartcards, cryptography or others to verify the person's identity or other information related to the transaction. Let's take a look. Technological verification tools are very simple in nature. The average technological means to help validate the consumer's identity or to confirm information associated with it. These tools can provide an additional layer of verification to help make sure that a consumer is the real person carrying out a transaction, and they can provide additional information such as tracking this specific device or placing the consumer at a specific location.

They usually, whether software such as cookies or cryptography or hardware such as smart devices, in order to achieve this goal. We are going to cover three main types of identity verification tools that leverage technology. The first is device or token identification. These are techniques that identify a device and that associate a user with that device for identification purposes using biometrics, USB dongles, smart cards, device cookies and others.

Then digital signatures are very simple using an electronic signature, usually relying on a private key of an asymmetric cryptography implementation to verify a consumer's involvement in a transaction and also provide non-repudiation so that they can't say that they didn't commit to the transaction. In finally consumer location, tracking a consumer via their cell phone location, GPOs, computer IP or others to put them at a specific place at a specific time. So as you see in this group of topics, we are going to cover how to use technological means of different types to verify information related to the transaction.

Technological Verification: Device/Token Authentication

Let's talk about device or token ID. This consists of verifying the person's identity through a physical means, such as a smartcard or a USB fob or a logical type of authentication, such as cookies or others. And these verify the person by verifying that specific device or token. Let's take a look. Authenticating a user through a device or token can provide an additional layer of security to the identity verification process. This can be done through a myriad of implementations, including first device identification, using a unique device identifier, either software or hardware to verify that divides in order to authenticate the transaction.

The very common type are cookies using browser information to identify a trusted device. Cookies are very cost effective because not only can they track a user across sites, they can also connect multiple devices and accounts to the same person. Then we have smart cards, physical cards that are used for authentication. Usually cards that have a chip just like credit or debit cards, but with different content. They're usually wrapped with a card reader. Then we have biometrics devices that range between. Fingerprint sensors to retinal scanners or others.

These are usually moderately to very expensive and not adopted in mass. They are for specific uses. For example, in the financial or health care industries, another common type are Ottps or One-Time passwords or whether tokens that are not passwords. These are one time codes or passwords that are sent via SMS or email, and they only work for that specific transaction within a very strict time frame. These techniques range in the level of complexity and protection that are involved, which by the way, are usually proportional. So for example, cookies are the cheapest but provide the least amount of security. While biometrics, such as retinal scanners, are usually the most expensive but also provide the most protection.

All other devices from smart cards to tokens to USB dongles in all other types fall somewhere in the middle when using device identification. One of the most important considerations is what equipment is necessary for the authentication. For example, both smartcard and biometric authentication have not been adopted on a larger scale due to the necessity of the consumer needing a card or a biometric reader. Because in order for a merchant to require these measures, every single one of their consumers must have that either or device. What are some examples? The first are retinal scanners. They are one of the most secure types, but also one of the most costly.

They are usually reserved for the medical, military or financial services markets. Just like voice authentication. Another example is government I.D. cards. In many countries, authentication can be performed using someone's government issued I.D. card, which has a chip. Granted that they have a card reader, Of course. Another example are cookies. Very simple and cheap. These can be used to easily identify a person. Can they be circumvented? Yes, but not easily. They take a lot of effort. They can also be used to track multiple accounts to one single device. What are our key takeaways here? The first is device identification. Any technique that consists of using software or hardware to identify the specific device associated with the user, which by association with that device authenticates the user.

Cookies, smart cards, biometrics and others. Another technique is using OTP one time passwords or unique codes that only work for a given transaction and that the user must enter to continue safe transactions. Finally, there are cost and security considerations for every one of these mechanisms because the different techniques vary in both the level of cost and the level of security provided when using them. So as we see, we can use several different types of authenticators in the physical or logical world, and they have different costs. But at the end of the day, what you're doing is authenticating a person through a device or a token.

Technological Verification: Digital Signatures

Let's talk about digital signatures. These are a form of electronic signatures, usually relying on cryptography that provide what is called non repudiation. That is, the association of the user with that signature is so strong that afterwards they can say that they weren't involved. Let's take a look at how it works. Digital signatures are a great way to apply an additional layer of consumer authentication and even non repudiation. In short, the consumer cannot claim to not have made the transaction if they have literally signed a document. They rely on the consumer using a digital signature that is based on cryptography.

They are the equivalent of real world signatures in many cases easier and faster to process. And in some cases, for example, documents such as contracts or specific industries such as financial services. These are actually required. Digital signatures vary in their implementation. They simply consist of encrypting a piece of information with a key, which is your private key, and anyone can use your public key to decrypt them. It's important to note that they may include or not a timestamp of the actual signature, which can be an important distinction for time sensitive or expiring documents.

Digital signatures usually rely on asymmetric cryptography, so the user has both a private key and the public one. So they sign with their private key. They encode the information in a way, and anyone can decode the information or read the signature with their public key. It's very simple. In other words, nobody knows the private key that was used to sign something, but they all know the public key that can be used to read it. This means that digital signatures are usually valid, but they can be rendered invalid in case of compromise of the person's private key that is used for their signature. What are some examples of digital signatures? The first are contracts or agreements.

Most high value purchases will include contracts or agreements that must be signed by the consumer, usually with this digital signature. Then you have signing platforms. Platforms like DocuSign are an alternative to a digital signature performed by you. You don't need to have the keys yourself. You just go, What do we sign a document in? They provide the signature themselves. The keys in your email are associated with their digital signature. And finally, specific sectors may require signatures, including most types of financial services, from loans and mortgages to investment products. What are our key takeaways? The first is that digital signatures are the equivalent of real world signatures, but they are digital and they are associated with the transaction.

They are based on cryptography. The user usually has both a public and a private key. They sign or encrypt information with their private key, and anyone can read the signature or decrypt the information with their public key. The public key is available to anyone, but the private key is exclusive to the person who signs that they can be compromised. It relies on asymmetric cryptography. Electronic signatures can be compromised if the person's private key is compromised itself. So as we see digital signatures provide a form of non repudiation, that is, the user can't say if they were not the ones to sign it. But remember, because they are based on cryptography, there is a way to break them, which is to compromise the private key.

Technological Verification: Consumer Location

Let's talk about consumer location. This consists of obtaining the person's location from a device, a proxy or the GPS or other means to place the user in a certain time during a transaction. It can be used to verify that a user was at a certain location or to corroborate with the location that you have on file and check for discrepancies. Let's take a look. Tracking the consumer's location at the time of the transaction can reveal some very interesting information and in many cases, fraudulent information. This location verification is usually performed in one of two major ways. The first is by tracking the person's IP or proxy.

This technique consists of attacking the person's device, IP location and in the case of a proxy being used the proxy address instead and checking whether that proxy is associated with fraudulent behavior, it's usually used as a support technique to verify the person's address and not by itself. The second method is for a mobile phone geo location tracking. This is a technique consisting of tracking a phone's location at the time of purchase. This location can then be compared to the shipping location of the transaction to possibly detect fraud. This is not just used for fraud detection, but for regulatory compliance.

In some industries, it's actually forbidden to make sales to certain territories. Both IP and mobile phone tracking are good, supporting information about a consumer's location, which may raise red flags in combination with other elements. For example, the transaction involves a shipping address in the U.S., but the full location is estimated in Russia, and the IP is using a known VPN proxy. This may indicate a suspicious account. These techniques are especially useful to the nai chargebacks by proving that the consumer was at a specific location at a specific time. It's important to note that in these cases, it's important to air on the side of the benefit of the doubt.

For example, it's not very useful to blacklist a proxy or a cell phone location due to one transaction, because there may be other multiple legitimate buyers that may be using the same proxy or that they have the same location. It's better to only hotlist the location or the proxy when you have a lot of hints from fraudulent transactions. What are some examples of consumer location? The first are streaming providers. If you've ever tried to read a Netflix show in specific and it says this is not available in your territory, they are using IP detection at play or possibly even tracking a proxy.

If you're using a commercial VPN, then mismatching information, different locations for the shipping address and the mobile phone may indicate a legitimate buyer who is traveling or on vacation. But they may also indicate if the transaction is important enough. The merchant or bank may call them to confirm the location and maybe do some sort of wallet checks. Both IP and mobile phone location services may vary in accuracy on average. They are usually stable, but there may be specific issues with specific parts of the world. What are our key takeaways here? The first is that the technique of

IP or proxy detection itself consists of detecting a consumer's location based on their device IP or if they're using a specific proxy or a VPN.

Detecting that, then the technique of phone number and location tracking tracks the physical location of the person's phone, and it may provide additional information about the phone itself with some providers. And finally, these are both used to place consumers at specific locations at specific times. These can be great for dispute resolution because they force the consumer to admit that they were at a specific location. But they're also good to detect fraud if there are inconsistencies. So as we see, there are many ways to calculate the person's location. But at the end of the day, you want to prove that they were in a certain place during the transaction.

Scores and Rules

Let's talk about scores and rules. That is both from scoring and business rules. Engines take information about a transaction and tell you what is the probability of it being fraud or they give you recommendations on results. But although they seem conflicting, you can actually use both for an optimized solution, but with a twist. Let's take a look at how both fraud, scoring and business rules are two important analytical systems that can integrate the different techniques. In other words, when you combine velocity checks, plot twists, device identification, you can combine them for use in a scoring system also known as a model based system, or combine them in a rules based system.

In many cases, ironically, scoring and rules are seen as being conflicting, but they are actually very effective in combination. So let's elaborate on business rules. These are simple conditions defining what to do for specific cases they follow. And if in logic, for example, if a $1,000 jewelry transaction is from a new client without a verified shipping address, manually review it. Or if a 250 transaction is from a hot listed credit card market. These are simple if then rules. Fraud scoring consists of using a model based system such as a neural network or a machine learning algorithm to attribute a score to a transaction, for example, from 0 to 1000. So you can have a neural network where you input the information 1000, usually a transaction from a new client with an unverified shipping address, and it returns a score of 850, for example, which is very risky.

It's not binary and it's more dynamic. For example, if the transaction was $900 instead of a thousand, maybe the score would be 800 instead of 850. Or if the shipping address was verified instead of unverified, maybe the score would be 500 instead of 800. And so one depending on the factors. Historically, fraud scoring has been used as an alternative to rules because in the past you either had a rules based system or a model based system. The latter came after and it soon arose in popularity because they are more flexible, especially against dynamic fraud. So a lot of people see rules as a conflicting system with fraud scoring, but in reality they can be used together.

Let me elaborate on how the recommendation is to have a model based system, which is also known as a behavioral system, because it models behavior that performs fraud scoring. But after that frog is scored, you can have additional operational rules on top of it. In short, you're not using the rules to fraud. You're using scoring to fraud and using rules afterwards to decide what happens with that score. For example, let's say that you have two transactions with a 900 rating. Very risky, but one is from a long term, high net worth individual client. It has been with you for a long time and the other one is from a new merchant.

This score may be the same, but do you handle both the same way as a bank? Absolutely not. Ideally, you want to have fraud scoring to the fraud with operational rules that come afterward to accommodate the different situations. They tell you whether to call or not. What type of analysts to assign? Whether to cue the investigation or any right now. And so one nowadays fraud scoring is then from model based, also known as behavioral systems but in specific, which are mostly optimized with artificial intelligence. All models must be dynamic nowadays because fraud is as well. Naturally, there are different types of AA models, including neural networks, machine learning and others.

But the key here is that these allow these behavioral models to not just be static, but instead evolve with changing conditions, especially for models that rely on artificial intelligence. It's imperative that the training data is of quality. If you know about it, you probably already know this by heart. If the training data is not of quality, the algorithm will not be either. Garbage in, garbage out. But for fraud monitoring mechanisms. There is a double problem here. Two distinct consequences. The first is the one that you're thinking of. Naturally, fraud is not detected. But the second problem, which may be even worse, is that fraudulent? Behavior as normal.

In other words, if you don't detect fraud, then that is normal behavior. So all fraud that comes afterwards that is similar will be considered normal behavior as well. What are some examples of scores and rules? The first is artificial intelligence. AI is frequently used with model based systems to improve the models in real time and is more and more trustworthy. Data comes in and refines the algorithm. The difference between scoring systems in rules engines is that the latter dictates a yes or no response in the form of if then rules. While model based systems allow for a gradual sliding scale scoring and finally, the usage of rules for operational decisions is another example.

As we mentioned, instead of using rules for scoring, we use them after the scoring to determine which type of analyst to assign, whether to cue the case or prioritize it among other elements. What are our key takeaways here? The first is the use of scoring versus rules for fraud. Historically, these have been the two major types of systems. Model based systems are more recent than rules based ones and have been more widely adopted because they're more flexible. The second takeaway is that rules should be used for the operations. With the advent of model based systems, rules have not been widely used for fraud detection itself, but they are still valuable.

After the front scoring for operational purposes. And finally, A.I. is used to improve the models in model based systems so that this model can remain up to date. Do new types of fraud appear? As we see, fraud scoring is more recent than business growth engines. But that doesn't mean that you need to discard the latter. You can use it for operations. And remember, it's always important to use artificial intelligence to keep up to date on the new fraud types.

Processes: Intro

Let's talk about processes. Processes are a group of fraud prevention techniques, which are actual processes within organizations such as insurance, menu reviewing cases and a lot more. Let's take a look at this group of topics. Processes, as the name says, are actual services provided by certain organizations, usually banks or card associations that can work as fraud monitoring techniques themselves. For example, having the bank call the consumer and verify their identity can be considered a technique despite also being a human process.

These naturally can be more costly than other froth prevention techniques, and they can take more time, but they can provide stability in additional layers of verification, especially by a third party due to their cost. In their complexity, they are usually reserved for high value transactions where it actually makes sense to use such costly techniques that their why is the actual value of the transaction. There's an offset to the costs in terms of process, we are going to cover two major types. The first is insurance and guarantees. These are services usually provided by insurers or payment platforms that either provide insurance against fraud or guarantee payment in case of fraud.

But they can place strict conditions on the merchant and the transactions that are covered. The second type are reviews and presentations. Manual reviews involve simply asking the bank to manually review a transaction while charging back. Re presentment consists of the merchant not contacting the client directly to solve a dispute, but having their bank contact the consumer's bank, which makes the process more official and easier to submit documents through. So as you see here, we are going to cover how actual processes from organizations can be used to prevent fraud.

Processes: Insurance and Guarantees

Let's talk about insurance and guarantees, that is payment, insurance and guaranteed payments. These help merchants in the case of fraud because they always get the money. But the problem is they're very strict and in many cases, they're also very costly. Let's take a look. There are two types of techniques that are useful for merchants dealing with consumers. Right. These are insurance policies and guarantees. Insurance, particularly e-commerce insurance, is a possible solution for merchants in case of fraud. They are reimbursed partially or totally. The problem here is that insurance can be very costly and on top of that, it can be restrictive in terms of what is.

In short, they may insure items only up to a certain value or we allow certain payment types. Each insurance policy is unique and specific and it may be worth the cost or not at all. Guarantees, including guaranteed payments, are another example. These are similar to insurance, but usually it's the payment processor that guarantees payment in case the consumer doesn't. For example, the only issue here is that, similar to insurance, they have requirements for eligibility which meet very strict requirements in terms of the type of transaction or the payment methods accepted due to the high costs and the specific requirements of both insurers and providers of guaranteed payments.

These options should be considered in case that a merchant wants stability. Let me elaborate. Because on one hand, they guarantee payment in case of fraud, which stabilizes income, but on the other hand, they also represent fixed costs which stabilize the expenses. They are options that should be very carefully analyzed in terms of risk and return, specifically in terms of what requirements the merchant must comply with in order to be eligible for insurance or payment. They may heavily restrict the types of cards or payments accepted, which will make the merchant restrict their business, and this can result in less orders. What are some examples of insurance and guarantees? The first is PayPal, an example of a guaranteed payment service.

If there is fraud, they will cover the amount, but the transaction must adhere to very specific guidelines. Another example is escrow services, the intermediate solution placing the funds in an escrow account. This allows that transfer to only occur on the waiver and automatically occurs on the waiver of the goods. And finally, specific issuers, some insurers or providers of guarantee payment mainly with payments to those, then with specific cards such as Visa or MasterCard, which then forces the merchant to do the same for their consumers and can represent less orders. What are our key takeaways here? The first is insurance, particularly e-commerce insurance. It allows merchants to be protected against fraud by letting them be reimbursed for a part or all of the damages.

Guaranteed payments used by some payment processors like PayPal guarantee the payment made even if the consumer defaults. But like insurance, they have strict rules. And finally, both of these are costly and strained. Both mechanisms have very strict rules in terms of which transactions are allowed and which aren't. They are also relatively costly. So as we see, these two techniques can be useful for a merchant if they're suffering from a large volume. But the problem is they're very strict and they may make the merchant result in a lot of transactions. So they have to be weighed very carefully.

Processes: Reviews/Representment

Let's talk about reviews and representative chapters. These are two processes which involve the merchant's bank in a situation either by manually reviewing the case or by acting in place of the merchant to represent them in terms of the dispute or the fraud case. But these are very costly and the results can vary a lot as well. So let's take a look at how these work reviews and write presentments are two processes specifically pertaining to the Merchants Bank that can help in situations of not just form but also disputes in general. Number one is that there are many reviews. This process consists of the bank staff manually reviewing a transaction.

It's a very costly technique, especially due to the fact that people are involved employees and it's best reserved for big transactions. For example, you would do a manual review if you get the down payment for a home for your bank, but you would probably never do it for a ten hour purchase of a book. The second is Chargeback RePresentment. This is a service provided by the bank that, in case of a dispute between a merchant and a cardholder, allows the merchant to be represented by them in conversation with the other bank. So the issuing in acquiring banks which represent the merchant and the consumer interface with each other.

Curiously, our presentment does not mean representation. The name comes from the fact that when a dispute occurs, both sides will be presenting evidence for the second time. So the bank will be doing a representative reference, also known as a second presentment. This allows the merchant to submit evidence in a structured manner by interfacing with a bank or insurer instead of dealing with a cardholder in private. The merchant goes through their bank so that they go to the cardholder's bank, to be honest. Both of these processes can vary greatly in terms of both the success, the time and the cost involved.

There are a lot of factors at play that determine the results, ranging from the experience level of the personnel involved, the relationships between the bank representatives, and honestly, just luck in the random factors. There are no guarantees and they should be avoided for lower value transactions because the transaction value doesn't even begin to offset the cost of this operation. So if the consumer buys a $200,000 car, makes a down payment and claims to never have bought it, the merchant can leverage these services, but for a 24 hour purchase of a book or maybe even a 201, these services just don't make up for it.

What are some examples of reviews and representations? But the first are mediation arbitration processes known as matter. These are two forms of dispute resolution mixed into one. Mediation means that a third party analyzes the situation and presents a solution. While in arbitration. The third party analyzes the situation and makes a legally binding decision that both parties must accept. Mediation, arbitration or method is a hybrid, so the third party can mediate the situation. And if the parties don't like the result, then the third party can then arbitrate and make the decision. In the case of re-presentment, for example, both banks are mediating and possibly arbitrating.

The second example is the use cases. These processes help with cases of fraud, but also other forms of dispute. Any type of situation where the merchant and the consumer are in these agreements. In the final case, management is an important related concept. Banks usually have organized processes to deal with these cases, which are known as case management processes or frameworks. These processes find the actions and the protocols to deal with the cases as well as the actual. Q What are our key takeaways? The first or many reviews consist of the merchant bank staff going over transaction data manually in order to try and draw conclusions. The second process is chargeback.

Representing the service provided by a bank allows a merchant to be represented by their bank in dialogue with a consumer's bank. They provide documents in evidence in a structured manner, which is known as the second presentment or the representation of the documents. And finally, both of these processes can be costly and have mixed results. They provide no guarantee of success, and they vary in terms of the costs and the results. So as we see both reviews and presentment, add more firepower. Involving a bank, usually the bank of the merchant. But the problem is they're very costly and the results are not guaranteed.

Fraud Prevention Techniques

We are now at the hands of the Fraud Prevention Techniques chapter where we cover so many techniques of different categories. Let's take a moment just to cover those different categories, as well as consolidate your knowledge with some questions. We are now at the end of the Fraud Prevention Techniques chapter where we covered different techniques of different categories. From this chapter, we covered five specific categories of fraud prevention techniques, all leveraging different methods or focusing on different aspects of the transaction.

The first group was data verification, using elements such as velocity checks, card checks and charge or deposit checks to verify information related to the transaction. Then identity verification techniques wastes automated lookups, manual authentication and or address verifications to try and verify the consumers identity. After that came technological verification. These are methods leveraging technology, such as smart devices or electronic signatures that provide an additional layer of identity verification. After that came scores and rules combining both fraud scoring and operational rules to improve fraud monitoring.

And after that, we touched on processes, services provided by banks or three parties that can be used as techniques to prevent or monitor fraud. Some questions that you can ask yourself to consolidate the knowledge in this chapter include What is the difference between an out of wallet check or out of pocket check and just calling the consumer to verify a transaction? What do they have in common and what's different about them? What kinds of devices can be used for authentication and what is their biggest barrier to adoption by consumers? On a large scale, insurance in guaranteed payments can stabilize the merchants cash, but they have several downsides.

Can you waste some of them? Do manual reviews guarantee that from what we discovered? What about chargeback representation for disputes? What kind of results do they achieve? What is the level of fraud detection provided by verifying yes, the billing address? And what about verifying the shipping address as well? And with this, we close the Fraud Prevention Techniques chapter where we try to cover all possible techniques to detect and prevent fraud.

Fraud Prevention Strategies Intro

We are now at the Fraud Prevention Strategies chapter. In this chapter, we are going to cover how to assemble a full fraud prevention solution. So we took a look at how fraud is committing the individual techniques to prevent it. And now we just have to assemble the system itself. Let's take a moment to review the topics and goals for this chapter. Welcome to the Fraud Prevention Strategies chapter, where we will cover considerations in assembling and optimizing a few from monitoring strategy. In terms of progress, we are now at the last chapter with three. We started by covering the different approaches to from who the different perpetrators are, what different strategies that use, and how fraud is executed in specific.

Then we covered different fraud prevention techniques, techniques used to verify identities, verify transaction data in leveraging different methods such as technology or even institutional processes. And now finally, we will cover fraud prevention strategies as a whole, how to select the techniques, how to use and process data and more. Our major goal in this chapter is simple. It's to take a look at how a fraud monitoring system is assembled and optimized. It includes topics such as how actual fraud monitoring data should be processed and stored for optimal functioning of the system.

What the actual key stages of fraud monitoring are, as well as what happens within each one of them, and how fraud monitoring techniques should be curated and combined based on the merchant or organization's risk and how to measure that risk. For this, we will cover four key topics related to fraud monitoring strategies. The first is covering the actual stages of fraud monitoring, which are usually five and what happens in each one of them. Then we will cover how to select and combine techniques for a full fraud monitoring solution based on the risk of the specific organization.

After that, we'll cover considerations in terms of data usage, making sure it scores in the reason codes are enforced and not tampered with, among others. Finally, data processing considerations, making sure that ETL processes don't delete data, that database changes are documented and more. So as you see in this group of topics, we are going to cover how to assemble a fraud prevention solution, how to maintain it, and how to optimize it.

Strategy Stages

Let's take a look at the different stages of a fraud prevention solution. This is important because some techniques operate at specific stages. For example, identity verifications are at an early stage pre transaction, but for example, many reviews of a fraud case by a bank are almost always at the analysis stage, which is a lot later. So let's take a look at the stages of fraud. Monitoring system usually has five major stages. The first three are usually automatic by nature, and they have to do with a transaction, pre transaction transaction and post transaction. The final two are usually manual and they have to do with the actual investigation and aftermath of the fright. The first stage is the pre-transaction stage.

It includes techniques such as rules or high twists. This is information that can flag or block a transaction before it even occurs. The second stage is the actual transaction. It involves techniques such as user authorisation or card security schemes. It validates user ID and other information and the actual time of purchase. The third stage is post transaction after transaction has been consummated. There are some checks that are performed, including front scoring in phone and address lookups that evaluate a transaction that has already occurred. The fourth stage is analysis.

This one is mostly manual. It may involve out of wallet checks, calling the consumer or other measures to try and find more evidence of fraud about a transaction that has already occurred. And finally, we have the conclusion stage. This is when all evidence has been collected and it's time to make one or more decisions. It may involve dispute resolution settlements between the merchant and cardholder tuning, the fraud strategy and possibly other measures. Usually the first three stages are automatic in nature, say four exceptions. While the two latter are manual in nature, we can split them into two parts, if you will. Prevention and investigation. So prevention consists of the first three stages.

Pre transaction transaction in both transactions. It's mostly about validating both the consumer's identity and account information. The transaction is either blocked or it may occur between the front score. The second part is the investigation, which consists of the analysis and conclusion stages. In this case, human capital is tasked with both reviewing the transaction and corroborating the information in it, possibly finding more evidence, and later drawing conclusions on what to do afterwards, depending on the urgency. This part can be done immediately after a transaction or it can be due for later treatment.

What are some examples of the different strategy stages? The first is whether something is automatic or manual. As mentioned, the first three stages related to the transaction are usually automatic, but they can be manual if the transaction merits it. For example, if an account has a hot, wasted credit card number, but it belongs to a high net worth individual, you may want to call them at the time of the transaction rather than blocking the transaction immediately. The second example is that the part that the analyst skills play does matter. The analyst allocated to the last two steps of the fraud case can impact the level of sophistication and the granularity of the data that you will obtain. So keep that in mind. And finally, integration counts.

Conclusions drawn from any fraud investigation should make their way back to the system as data. I would argue they must make their way back there because if they don't, a lot of this process is useless if the information isn't fees and artificial intelligence systems, for example, you learned nothing from this fraud investigation. Our key takeaways include. First, there are five stages in any fraud monitoring strategy pre transaction doing the transaction in both transactions which are usually automatic and for prevention. Then analyses and conclusions which are usually manual and are about investigation. The first three stages, the prevention phase are mostly automatic, as we covered, while the following to the investigation are mostly manual.

And finally, there is a bigger context at play while the strategy itself counts. There are many other elements in 20, such as analyst skills and data feedback that also match. For fraud detection. So as you see, we have several stages of a transaction in a fraud monitoring solution. And it's important to note these because different techniques operate at different stages. But also remember that not only the techniques themselves, but other factors such as analyst skill, define how well you actually prevent fraud.

Technique Considerations

Waits took a look at technique considerations. That is, when you're assembling a fraud prevention solution. How do you pick the different techniques? It usually comes down to two factors: the volume of the transactions and the sensibility, or the ease of reselling of the actual product. But there is a lot more to this. So let's cover it. When finding a strategy, the techniques included should not be selected blindly, but based on the fraud risk of the specific retailer or organization. Some techniques such as address verification, credit card checks and others are fast and cheap, while others, such as biometric authentication or manual chalk reviews, are expensive and time consuming. So knowing which ones to use is very important.

So when selecting the tools to assemble a full strategy, the organization has to select them based on the time and effort involved with each. Organizations can usually be categorized as a low, medium or high risk, and it mostly comes down to two factors, which are the volume of transactions and the sensibility of the goods. So for low risk, we have retailers or merchants that have low volume and whose goods have a low sensibility or none at all. This includes goods such as clothing, tuition, insurance and other personal products. They are not easily accessible. People can sell them for money very easily. Then we have medium risk. These are merchants with medium to high volume and whose goods have medium to high fence ability.

They can be sold somewhat easily. Think of toys, games, music, books, clothing or travel. And finally, we have high risk, which usually comes down to high volume and high sensitivity of goods. This is usually the case for electronic downloads, gift cards, adult products, gaming, disposable cell phones, credit lines, or consumer electronics such as computers or smartphones. These levels of risk, given the types of techniques that we should use, there are some that are universal. They should be used at all levels. These include address verification, card security schemes, the velocities of use in velocities of change and consumer identification. These should be used in all three battles.

Then specifically for low risk merchants, you can use, for example, net address lookups or email and phone verification. This is what you see when you register for a clothing retailer online, for example. For medium risk merchants, you should use front scoring and rules engines. This is what you will see, for example, in travel portals or high end clothing stores. Finally, we have high risk merchants. You should use front scoring in rules engines with II to help the models evolve. You should consider wallet checks, device ID or some sort of biometrics, and you can also consider insurance or guarantees.

This is used, for example, for online casinos, financial products or the adult industry. What are some examples of technique considerations? The first is matching costs. Technique selection should be based on the level of risk due to the expected costs. This is why for low value merchants with low face ability where there is not going to be a lot of impact due to fraud, the measures can be basic with a low cost. But for high volume merchants with high visibility, the impact of fraud will be very high. So costly techniques are justified. The techniques should always depend on the actual expected costs of fraud. In general, automated is always cheaper than manual. Of course, there are exceptions.

There are very expensive automated processes and there are manual processes with people. They have a lot of expertise in doing things fast. But this is the general rule. Also, make sure the techniques match the design to the actual cost of individual techniques. Make sure that these are integrated into a unified system. You should have the right techniques, but also combine them the right way. If you have 50 techniques but they don't share information, they are pretty much useless. The right techniques must combine. Right? What are our key takeaways here? The first is that there are mostly three groups of risk: low, medium and high technique. Selection is mostly defined by this. Then the criteria for defining the risk of those three groups is usually defined by two factors: the volume of the goods and their sensitivity to how easily they can.

Be sold. The risk level is merely a factor of one times the other. And finally, it's a balancing act when assembling techniques. Some are going to be more expensive or time consuming, but they detect more froth. And it's important to make sure that you balance the time or cost consumed and the quality of protection. So as we see, we can usually group organizations into three major levels of risk low, medium and high. And it usually depends on the volume of transactions and visibility of the goods. But it's important to be aware of the specific nature and the specific needs of your organization when assembling a solution, because there are always tradeoffs at the end of the day.

Data Usage Considerations

Let's talk about data usage considerations. That is, it is very possible to have a full fraud prevention solution so miserably if people don't respect the data or don't record data in the first place. So let's take a look at some best practices in terms of data usage, assuming that you have a model based system that's causing fraud. But even if you have an author, rule rules based on one data is crucial. And for systems that leverage artificial intelligence in order to learn, this is even more important. Some guidelines for data usage include. First of all, you have to enforce that fraud scoring is used.

What I mean by this is front scoring is useless if it's not respected, if a transaction is flagged as a 950, for example, which is very high, but the analyst decides to override the score, then the fraud monitoring system is pretty much useless. In other words, fraud scoring is not a recommendation. It's something that is sacred and that analysts must obey and they can make operational decisions afterwards, but that doesn't contradict the score. In short, if people don't obey the scores, it's useless to have them in the first place. The second consideration is that scores and reason codes must be recorded both the reason Codes for Chargebacks, for example, the Visa and MasterCard ones, and the front scoring must be used and recorded by all team members.

If the previous point was about what an analyst takes, then this point is about what the output. Mainly analysts are not strict in terms of documenting the reason codes and the front scores. So you end up with fraud cases where there is no documentation, or at least that information is not granular enough to use in the future. You have to consider this from an I.D. point of view, a database point of view. It doesn't matter how good the analyst's intentions are. If the database field is not saved, if the information isn't there, then this case doesn't exist. The fraud monitoring system will learn nothing from it. This is why recording both the fraud scores and the reason codes is so important. It must be a process happening in every case so that the monitoring system can learn from every case. Finally, fraud data must always be reported.

There are some cases where it's not even a matter of the scores or the reason codes. It's even worse. The actual case is not documented in the system. This happens for both fraud and just transactions themselves. All transactions, including fraudulent ones, must be recorded. And if there is any database issue, be aware of the faulty or deleted data as well. Document the losses. So recording fraud data must not be an option, but a mandatory process both in terms of what is present but also what is missing. Everyone in the team must know exactly what transactions are in the database in which they are missing, period. You may think that these guidelines may seem so obvious and even naive, but you would be surprised at how many institutions don't follow them.

You have fraud cases that are not reported that have missing scores, or there's a system blackout that doesn't record the transaction information for a couple of hours or even days. And nobody knows about this. So, for example, maybe the bank uses fraud scoring, but only as a recommendation. So the analysts are the ones that end up defining how serious a transaction is, including those that have no experience or in many cases, the reason codes are just not recorded. This results in having multiple transactions where the merchant doesn't provide or can't provide the documentation because they don't even know what type of dispute it is in the first place. And if your bank has to do a re-presentment with the other bank, that's even worse.

That's a problem for you as well. In many cases, transaction data is not even recorded seriously. Sometimes data problems occur and there is no indication of what data is missing or how many transactions. This makes historical reviews difficult or even impossible. What are some examples of data usage considerations? The first is having absolute trust in the system that the institutions with the highest fraud detection rate assemble a good system and then put. Absolute trust into the score and they leave it. Animists should never try to outsmart the system or override it. Then recording data in usage of scores and codes should be a systematic process.

The only way to make sure that it's always done is to enforce it automatically as a process. Time after time, data integrity is another example. The best systems need quality data to work with, even when data is missing. They know what they don't know. Missing data is as important as present data. What are our key takeaways? The first is that you have to respect the score. Once you've assembled a quality system that generates front scores. Don't get in your own way. Stressed the score in forcing employees to do so as well. Make sure to enforce any of the scores and the reason codes.

All members of the fraud monitoring team must both enforce the scores and the reason codes. Otherwise there will be no consistency in transaction data in the system. Can't even use those data and finally always report they're the one that's there and the one that's missing. Recording the fraud review decisions in especially the raw transaction data is not an option. It's a necessity for an efficient system in AI systems to depend on this constant data to a fault. So as you see, there are many things to take into account, but at the end of the day it's about making sure that you record information such as reason codes and fraud scores in respecting the system, because you can have the best system in the world. But if its conclusions are not respected, you may as well not have it.

Data Processing Considerations

Let's talk about data processing considerations. That is, there are certain processes within a company such as ETL processes that can destroy the quality of data or lower it. If you are a data management expert, you probably know this by heart. It's all about ensuring data quality according to certain dimensions. But for the uninitiated, don't panic. We are going to cover some quick tips on how to not let certain processes destroy your data. Let's take a look. Besides, in terms of actual usage of fraud monitoring data, there are also important considerations and guidelines in terms of how it's processed and stored. First of all, additions and changes to the database must be documented and planned for ahead of time.

Additions to the data schema must be planned for in the database and they must be documented. There are many cases of instances where the data architect makes a change to the schema. They warn no one. They don't document it, and nobody in the institution has any idea of what this field means. In many cases, what happens is that people try to derive the meaning from the filename, which sometimes it's obvious but sometimes is impossible to decipher. For example, you have a few Hawkwind types that may be an enumeration from 1 to 5 in a car type that is an enumeration from 1 to 6.

And suddenly, for some reason, the client type field is extinguished, maybe because it's not needed anymore, or it changed the format and the system is going to start storing the data in the car type field. If this is documented, then people know that they can interpret the data this way and everything is fine from that date onwards. Ignore this field and use the other one. But if this is not documented, it will be an unmitigated disaster. You are going to have bogus data on all client times in transactions and you have no idea why or even when it changed. This is how important it is to document and plan for changes in the database. Another point is that real time integration is crucial.

What I mean by this is, if any data that the fraud monitoring system cannot access in real time is useless, it may as well not be there. There are many institutions where data from various departments or systems is not usable, or maybe it's usable, but through an API that takes time and has limits. The bottom line is all systems must be interconnected and see the solution in real time. The data must be usable and must be accessible in real time. If it's not in the eyes of the system, it doesn't even exist. As simple as that. And finally, be very aware of ETL simplifications. ETL processes must not simplify data.

But unfortunately, that's precisely what they do in many institutions. Otherwise, the data is going to be granular in the operational database, but not in the data warehouse. To give you an example, let's say that you're storing a reason code, for example, 10.3 in the database. So you have both yields in the operational database, the ten and the three. But in the data warehouse, the three is truncated in only the ten remains. So you will want to run from analysis and suddenly you'll find that the data in the operational database is complete. But all of the historical data in the data warehouse is rubbish, or at least is limited because it has been simplified.

So in that case, you know the general purpose of the reason code, but you don't know its specific reason which is symbolized by a three. So that's the chapter here. ETL processes must not oversimplify data. All of these different principles reflect a bigger and more important guideline, which is that the fraud monitoring system must have real time access to granular data in order to do its job in granular data that is complete. Anything that is a threat to this is a threat to the system. So data that doesn't exist is not usable. Of course, data that exists but is not available in real time is not usable. Data that exists and it is available in real time but is simplified and is not granular. It is not usable. You can see where I'm going with this.

The fraud monitoring system is only as strong as its weakest link, so every weak link must be reinforced. Every type of incomplete or inaccessible data must be made available in real time. Then the system will work dramatically better. What are some examples of data processing considerations? The first is mergers and acquisitions. When banks are. Merged or acquired different departments with different DB schemata are merged as well. If these are not integrated right away, they will be useless to the fraud monitoring system. Another example is a numerical oversimplification. Water just covering an ideal process may take random miracle data and simplify it. So a recent code that is 10.3 in the database is only saved as a ten in the data warehouse.

Remember, raw information is always better, and finally, real time is crucial. Don't forget the real time in real time integration data that cannot be accessed right away is useless because even if you could access it later, the froth may already happen in the meantime. What are our key takeaways here? The first is that any changes to the database fields must merit documentation that everyone has access to. Nothing is worse than not knowing what you have. Second real time is crucial since fraud monitoring is a real time endeavor. Information must be accessible in real time. Otherwise, it's just plain useless. Inferred ETL processes must not be destroyed.

In many cases, there is a different schema between the database and the data warehouse. And it's not a good difference because ETL processes end up removing part of the information when they stop it. You need to make sure that this doesn't happen. So as you see, these are just some tips to achieve what could be called data quality hygiene, documenting changes, making sure the data are available in real time. And so on. Because remember, if they're not available in real time, they're useless.

Fraud Prevention Strategies

We are now at the end of the Fraud Prevention Strategies chapter where we try to cover how to assemble, maintain and optimize a fraud prevention solution. Let's take a moment to cover the topics that we took a look at, as well as consolidate your knowledge with some questions. We are now at the end of the Fraud Prevention Strategies chapter, where we covered different considerations in terms of assembling and optimizing a front monitoring strategy. In order to cover these, we touched on four key topics. The first was the mention of the five different stages of a fraud monitoring strategy, as well as what happens within each of them. The second or third considerations in terms of the techniques to be selected based on the risk level, the merchant organization, and how to calculate it.

After that, we touched on considerations in terms of usage, including enforcing score in reasoned code usage and documentation. And finally, we covered considerations in terms of data processing itself, including documenting database changes and not letting ETL processes remove data, among others. Some questions that you can ask yourself to consolidate the knowledge in this chapter include First is fraud scoring respective by my institution? Or can analysts or other team members just overwrite a score and ignore it? Then there's the technique selection for my organization's risk level that matches the recommended techniques.

Do they offset the frost costs? Are they cost effective results? How is information being stored? Are ETL processes oversimplifying? Data is missing data recorders are database schema changes planned for and properly documented? Do I know the five stages of fraud monitoring intimately? How does my organization handle each one of them? Automatically? Manually? Which techniques do they use in each stage? And with this, we close the Fraud Prevention Strategies chapter, where we try to cover how to assemble, maintain and optimize a full fraud prevention solution.

What Next

We are now at the end of our Introduction to Fraud Prevention Book. Congratulations on reaching so far. Let's take a moment to recap the three chapters that we've covered throughout this Book. We aim to cover the fundamentals of fraud and prevent specific payments from. For this purpose we covered topics including first which types of actors performed prior, what motivations each one of them has, and how they do it. Then what the different executions of RA have in common as well as how they are detected. After that, we covered an exhaustive list of fraud prevention techniques that validate data identities and use methods ranging from technology to pure data to human processes.

And finally, we took a look at how to combine different fraud prevention techniques to make a full strategy based on this specific organization's risk level, as well as how to optimize the system in terms of both data and people in order to achieve this. We covered three key chapters in this Book. The first were approaches to fraud. We covered the different types of fraud that are committed as well as by who and what the execution looks like in detail. Then it was all about the techniques, techniques to validate identities, account information and other transaction elements using data, manual checks, processes, technology and more.

And finally, our third chapter was about how to assemble a fraud monitoring strategy based on techniques, as well as how to optimize it with people and data. We closed that introduction to the fraud prevention Book. I hope this Book has helped you professionally in giving you more information on how fraud is performed and how to stop it. Thank you so much for reading. And with this, we close the introduction to the fraud prevention Book. Thank you so much for reading.

Payment Risk and Payment Fraud: Data Science and Analytics

Hello and welcome to Introduction to Dispute Resolution. In this Book we are going to cover everything related to disputes. We are going to focus on payment disputes, but all of the knowledge that you amass here can be used for other types of disputes as well. Without further ado, let's take a look at the chapters and topics of this Book. Hello and welcome to Introduction to Dispute Resolution, where we are going to cover everything related to resolving disputes, especially involving payments. So in this Book we have a major goal, which is to cover the essentials of dispute resolution, how to resolve disputes, what are the processes, what are the requirements and how it's done. And especially in payment disputes that always involve some sort of merchant or seller on one end and the cardholder or buyer on the other end in their respective banks in many cases.

So we are going to cover in more detail many different topics, including, for example, how IVR or alternative dispute resolution differs from litigation. What are its advantages as well? Is the different implementations of IVR or what the OCR or online dispute resolution framework consists of resolving disputes with the use of electronic means as well as its main principles and some use cases, or, for example, how dispute resolution occurs for merchant clients on the part of an acquiring or merchant bank. That is, if you are the bank of a merchant who is involved in a dispute, what do you do?

Including the usual life cycle of a dispute, the circumstances for the possible involvement of the payment scheme and general guidelines.

For example, in finally a big portion of the whole Book is going to be about the usual reason codes for chargebacks in payments from issuing banks as well is what measures a merchant in the recurring bank can do in the face of each in back to the Book structure in terms of the Book itself, to properly cover everything related to dispute resolution, we are going to touch on four key chapters. The first is about approaches to ADR or alternative dispute resolution. We'll cover the three main ones negotiation, mediation and arbitration, as well as the pros and cons and specific implementations. Next comes O the R or online dispute resolution. How do you solve disputes using electronic means? What principles does it rely on and how is it implemented? Then we'll cover dispute resolution for merchant banks or acquiring banks, as they're also called in specific ways to deal with disputes involving your merchant clients.

General guidelines, an overview of the process and more. And finally, we'll dive deep into the reason codes for chargebacks, which are possible by issuing banks during a dispute which involves a chargeback. We'll cover the four main types which are fraud, authorisation errors, processing errors and consumer disputes, as well as dozens of reason codes within those in what merchants or acquiring banks should do when facing each individual reason code. So as you see in this Book, we are really going to cover everything related to disputes, the chargeback reason codes, the ADR approaches, and a lot more.

Dispute Considerations

Let's cover some considerations and terminology related to disputes. Before going deeper, it's important to know what is actually the dispute and the different types of disputes. So let's take a look at some definitions when talking about disputes and in particular payment disputes. It's important to clarify some concepts first. First of which is the difference between fraud and the dispute. Disputes can be considered any disagreement between two parties and in payment disputes, they usually occur between the merchant and the card holder or the consumer. These are the two parties usually involved in any payment. So fraud is merely one of the reasons for these disputes.

So if a card is stolen or used without authorization, that is from out of curiosity, besides cardholder froth with the stolen card or with a counterfeit card. The merchant themselves may also be the one to commit fraud by charging a different amount, extra transactions or others. But it's important to state that there are other reasons for disputes which are not from. These may include authorization errors, processing errors, or consumer disputes where the consumer and the merchant disagree on the expectations about a product. All of these represent disputes, but fraud is only one type of them. When talking about disputes, it's also important to draw the distinction between contractual and non-contractual disputes.

Contractual disputes are any type of dispute where there is a contract or agreement between two parties. Non-contractual disputes are cases where there is no contract or agreement or even any relationship between two parties as payment disputes are caused by a transaction. They are therefore considered contractual disputes. It's important to realize that contractual disputes don't necessarily need a contract. They are based on the agreed upon terms. In this case, the terms of a transaction which may be stated at the time of purchase on a web page or possibly in an actual contract if there is one.

So if you buy something online, then you have the terms of service for that seller on a web page. And there is a dispute that is a contractual dispute, and the terms are the ones that the seller has right out of curiosity. Non-contractual disputes also exist, although payment disputes are not of this type. Non-contractual disputes occur when there is no relationship between the parties. So, for example, IP infringement or trademark infringements, among other actions, are not bound by a contract or even any relationship between the two parties are classified as non-contractual disputes. What are some examples of dispute considerations? The first is a stolen car.

If a consumer starts a dispute due to their car being stolen and used by someone else. This is both a dispute and the case of fraud in the process known as a chargeback, which will occur where the issuing bank of that card will ask for the money back to the acquiring bank or the merchant bank representing the merchant. If a consumer opens a dispute due to the fact that a product's quality is not what was stated, that is considered a dispute, but it's not fraud. It's merely a consumer dispute. And finally, as we stated, all payment disputes are usually contractual disputes because there is some sort of agreement between both parties about what is expected of that purchase. And there are mutual expectations. What are our key takeaways here? The first is that payment disputes usually occur between a merchant and the consumer or cardholder in case that the banks are involved.

The merchant is represented by the merchant or acquiring bank, while the cardholder or consumer is represented by the issuing bank. They issue the card from a dispute that is not necessarily equivalent. Disputes occur for a myriad possible reasons and fraud is simply one of them. Authorization hours processing errors in consumer disputes are other possible types, and finally, payment disputes are usually considered contractual disputes. There may not be an explicit contract between both parties, but there is an agreement about what to expect from each side. So as we see, disputes are not the same as fraud. They are just in general any type of disagreement and usually in a transaction in specific between a merchant and the cardholder.

Air Or Alternative Dispute Resolution

Let's cover air or alternative dispute resolution approaches. In this chapter, we are going to cover ADR. In ADR it is simple. Any type of dispute resolution which does not involve courts because historically every dispute was solved in courts. So everything which does not involve litigation is considered IPR. Let's take a moment to cover the topics and goals for this chapter. In this chapter, we are going to cover the different types of AVR or alternative dispute resolution and the various implementations of it. But take a look at our progress so far. Right now we're right at the beginning and the first chapter A4. In this chapter, we will cover the different types of ADR for alternative dispute resolution.

So dispute resolution methods that are not litigation. In the second chapter, we will cover the OCR or online dispute resolution framework, its context, its principles and how it is implemented. In the third chapter, we will cover merchant banking and specific the process flow for disputes both for issuing and acquiring banks, as well as operational optimizations of these processes. And finally, will cover the different reason codes for Chargebacks. When an issuing bank requests a chargeback. Usually there is a reason code associated. We will explore the major categories, the reason codes as well as the measures that merchants should take in the face of these.

What are our goals for this chapter? The major one is simple, which is to cover the different types of alternative dispute resolution or ADR in more detail. We will cover which ADR processes are considered consensual and which are considered adversarial. We'll cover the different types of processes that are usually grouped into three major types. Negotiation, mediation and arbitration. We will cover the advantages of ADR approaches versus litigation, and we will cover situations for which the different ADR types are recommended for this purpose. We are going to cover the three main types of ADR approaches. The first is negotiation.

This involves an approach where both parties negotiate among themselves and reach a conclusion without any intervention from a third party. Then we'll cover mediation. These are approaches that involve a third party suggesting a resolution for both sides, but not enforcing that resolution. And finally, we will cover arbitration. These are approaches that involve a third party finding a resolution for both parties in making a decision that is binding for both parties. So as we see in this chapter, we are going to cover three types of ADR in specific as well as their benefits and drawbacks.

Negotiation

Let's cover negotiation. Negotiation means the two parties resolving the dispute among themselves. It's the equivalent of a teacher telling two problematic school kids, Hey, just fix it among the two of you. I'm not going to be involved. It's very fast food because it doesn't require a third party. But that is also one of the major drawbacks. So let's take a look at negotiation. Negotiation is a form of alternative dispute resolution where both parties reach an agreement on their own. Both parties negotiate voluntarily among themselves, and there is no third party involved. This is actually usually the most frequent type of dispute resolution because it's the fastest and it's the least costly.

And surprisingly, because there is no time or cost involved with any mediator or any arbitrator, because both parties just resolve the dispute among themselves. Negotiation is usually informal in nature and mediation or arbitration. There are no formal rules. There is no structure governing it. Both parties just negotiate as they see fit. They make an offer, a counteroffer, and they go back and forth. Negotiations can be balanced in terms of power between both parties or not at all. In many cases, negotiation is preferred because it's the most flexible format known that both parties need to obey rules or structures that are imposed by mediator or arbitrator instead of having to attend a certain amount of meetings or show a certain amount of evidence and present it to analysis.

You simply tell the other side what you have in what you want, and you go back and forth with them. This is also the type of ADR that tends to generate more successful outcomes because both parties are working together as opposed to involving a third party. It's important to notice, though, if negotiation can be however unfair, especially when both parties have an equal power. This may cause the weaker party to not be properly represented if the other one has a lot more resources and power. Negotiation is also not ideal if both parties cannot reach a mutual understanding of the problem, or if they simply do not agree on it.

If they have fundamental differences of opinion, what are some examples of negotiation? The first are unfair dynamics. Negotiation may not work when one party, as they want more power than the other one, may just stall them or refuse to see their point of view. Second, the lack of structure in negotiation means that any of the two parties can just drop out at any time. Or it can suggest reasonable solutions. And there is no protection against either situation. The flexibility of negotiation is both its biggest strength, but also its biggest weakness. And finally, negotiation results in true collaboration, at least when it's been well and when it works.

Negotiation can generate results for both parties because they are both operating in their joint interests and they can maintain a healthy relationship. What are our key takeaways here? The first is that negotiation is quick and efficient. It's the quickest, the least costly in the most efficient type of alternative dispute resolution, at least when it's well executed. Second, negotiation maintains good faith. It requires the cooperation of both parties, which means that good faith between them is maintained in a successful negotiation, each looking out for the interests of both.

And finally, negotiation is not moderated, which is simultaneously its biggest strength, but also its biggest weakness. The fact that there is no third party makes it more flexible, faster, and costly. But it also means that nobody can mediate emotional or incompatible disputes which can result in stalemates. So as we see, negotiation is quick and efficient because the two parties just get in touch and fix it between themselves. But the problem is because there is no third party. There may be power imbalances between these two.

Mediation

Let's talk about mediation. Mediation is a type of ADR where a third party comes in and evaluates the situation, but they don't make any binding decision. In fact, that's the difference between mediation and arbitration. If they evaluate the situation but make a decision as well, that's arbitration. But there are different types of mediation available. So let's take a look at how it works. Mediation can be considered any type of dispute resolution that involves a third party giving their opinion on a dispute or analyzing the situation, but not making a decision themselves. As the name says, they only mediate the situation. There are many specific implementations of mediation, which include first neutral evaluations.

These are situations where a third party evaluates the evidence in the arguments of both sides. They are usually technical in nature because the mediator must have technical knowledge so that they can properly analyze the situation. Another example are settlement addresses, which are situations where both parties sit with a judge that takes a look at both sides' evidence and arguments, and suggests a settlement for the situation but does not actually enforce it or make any decision. And finally, another variation are review boards. These are boards that are usually composed of three people, three different mediators, and that all give their impartial look as a group on a dispute.

In some cases, within mediation, there is a distinction drawn between facilitation and evaluation. These can be considered two different types of mediation. Facilitation is about only helping both parties communicate. While evaluation involves an actual analysis of this situation. So facilitation is less formal and it's more about assisting both parties as they communicate instead of formally analyzing the situation. Evaluation itself is a more formal process where, well, as the name says, there is a formal evaluation of the situation according to a set of criteria, maybe following a specific process in evaluating the evidence and the arguments of both sides.

This usually also requires technical expertise on the part of the mediator or expert for the disputes that actually require them to have this technical knowledge. Naturally, both types are considered mediation by definition, because in both there is a third party that helps but does not enforce a solution. What are some examples of mediation? The first is involving an expert mediator. If a merchant and consumer cannot negotiate among themselves, then they may request an expert mediator to suggest a path forward. The second example is bank mediation. If a merchant in a cardholder cannot negotiate among themselves with their banks, where we usually do it for them, the acquiring for a merchant bank representing the merchant and the issuing bank representing the cardholder.

This is considered mediation by these banks. There are also situations where the banks cannot reach a settlement. So the payment scheme is involved in the enforcing solution. In that case, there is arbitration instead of mediation. And finally, a hybrid example is mediation. Arbitration, also known as math R in this hybrid model. The mediator starts by suggesting the solution. And if the parties still don't accept the solution, then that third party can arbitrate making a binding decision. So it goes from mediation to arbitration. What are our key takeaways here? The first is that in mediation there is no decision. It's a type of alternative dispute resolution where a third party analyzes the situation and presents a possible solution to both sides. But that's all they do.

Second, there may be multiple formats. The third party may be an individual expert, a board or any other type, as long as they mediate the dispute and present a solution. And finally, mediation can usually be categorized into facilitation or evaluation. Facilitation is just about guiding communication among both parties informally, while evaluation involves a formal analysis of the situation. So as we see, mediation is all about having a middle person who comes in and just evaluates the situation. But they can also only facilitate the communication between both sides. So there are different levels of involvement from aviation. But at the end of the day, it's any type of ADR where a third party comes in, evaluates the situation, but does not make any decision.

Arbitration

Let's talk about arbitration. Arbitration is a type of ADR where an objective third party comes in, evaluates the situation, but also makes a binding decision. It's almost like a court process, but more fluid and less formal. But there are different types of arbitration, and there are different circumstances which can affect how effective it is. So let's take a look. Arbitration is a type of alternative dispute resolution where a neutral third party acts as a private judge for the situation. Imposing a resolution for it that is a legally binding arbitration is usually done with the selection of a neutral judge. So either both parties select one arbitrator together or there is a panel of three, for example, where each side selects one arbitrator and then these two together select a third one.

For example, arbitration has several advantages, including the fact that it's neutral in terms of nationality and law. It's confidential in terms of the information shared, and it's easy to enforce without the weight or complication, as opposed to negotiation and mediation, which are considered consensual processes because both parties reach a conclusion together. Arbitration is considered adversarial because the arbitrator must be the one to impose a resolution because both parties cannot agree on one. Arbitration can be particularly useful when the issue requires technical knowledge because both parties can select the appropriate court and judge if they do possess that technical knowledge.

And it's also faster than traditional litigation. It's not without its downsides, though, and there can be, for example, limited avenues for appeals because it's not a formal trial. And also, in the case of partial corporations that choose the arbitrators, if they provide repeat business for them, then the arbitrators may have a reason to rule in their favor. What are some examples of arbitration? The first is that, in fact, the arbitrator may have been pre-selected in some consumer agreements or contracts. The arbitrator may be predefined in the fine print or in the hidden costs. This is dangerous because the arbitrator that is predetermined may be one that is favorable to the merchant. Naturally, another example are technical courts. Arbitration is useful because for highly technical issues, both parties can select a specific court, an arbitrator that can properly evaluate the situation.

And finally, arbitration can have a variable duration, although my principle, it's shorter on average than traditional litigation. If there are multiple arbitrators involved, each one of them with their own schedule, there may be scheduling conflicts in other elements which can affect the process and result in more costs. What are our key takeaways here? The first is that arbitration consists of a third party deciding whether one arbitrator or a panel of them decides on a resolution to a dispute that is legally binding and enforceable. Second, it's neutral and confidential, at least in most cases. This allows for a quicker decision than what would happen in traditional courts.

And finally, there may be specific issues with arbitration that affect insufficiency. For example, predetermined clauses in contracts that choose the arbitrator or arbitrators that do repeat business with some corporations. So as we see in arbitration, the third party both evaluates the situation but also makes a decision. It's usually confidential and it's usually neutral, and there are specialties for ADR. But it's important to notice that the contract clauses themselves can affect how effective IVR actually is.

Recap

We are now at the end of the eight year approaches chapter. Let's think for a moment just to recap the three types of ADR as well as consolidate our knowledge with some questions. We are now at the end of the ADR Approaches chapter where we cover the different types of alternative dispute resolution or ADR in their various implementations. In this chapter, we explore the three main types of alternative dispute resolution approaches. The first was negotiation approaches. They involve both parties reaching a conclusion among themselves with no third party involved. The second was mediation approaches that involve a third party suggesting a resolution for both sides, but not making a decision.

And finally, arbitration approaches that involve a third party making a binding decision for both parties. Some questions that you can ask yourself to consolidate the knowledge in this chapter include within mediation. What is the difference between facilitation and evaluation? In which situations is arbitration passed and in which is it late? What is the difference between mediation and arbitration and what happens in a mediation, arbitration or math R process? Which two ADR types are considered consensual? In which one is considered adversarial? And finally, why is arbitration chosen over litigation for technical disputes? With IS we close the ADR Approaches chapter where we try to cover every type of dispute resolution, which is not litigation.

OCR or Online Dispute Resolution

We are now at the OCR or online dispute resolution chapter. In this chapter we're going to cover how disputes are resolved through electronic means. This may seem basic, right? Let's just solve the dispute for the internet, but there are certain requirements and certain principles in order for any electronic platform to be considered trustworthy. Let's take a moment to cover the topics and goals for this chapter. Welcome to the online Dispute Resolution chapter, where we are going to cover the overlap framework. It's context in its different implementations. Before proceeding, let's just gauge our progress for a minute. We are now in the second chapter. What for? First, we cover the different ADR approaches negotiation, mediation, arbitration and specific implementations of these three. Now we are in the online dispute resolution chapter.

We are going to cover what ADR is, what it consists of in space principles, in how it's implemented, in specific. Then we're going to cover how dispute resolution works in merchant banking, the types of disputes involving your merchant clients, the oral process, and the possible involvement from the payment scheme. And finally, we are going to cover in detail the possible reason codes for chargebacks in payment disputes. What the different types of reason codes represent as well is what to do in those cases. Our major goal in this chapter is to cover what OCR is and how it's implemented.

More in detail, we are going to cover what the three usual steps of an OCR procedure are, as well as the three categories or the are tools, electronic negotiation, electronic mediation and electronic arbitration work as well as specific implementations. That is how litigation itself, besides ADR, can also be done through OCR, through the use of cyber courts. Also, what these six key principles of an effective OCR platform are and what are some specific implementations in case studies, the different OCR tools as well as the reasons for their working. In order to achieve this. We are going to explore three key topics in terms of OCR.

The first is the context in principles of OCR, how it came about and what it represents. Then we'll cover the steps and the categories and the usual steps in an over the hour procedure as well as the three major categories or tools. Finally, we'll cover different implementations in case studies of OCR for specific purposes. So as you see in this chapter, we are going to cover how to properly solve disputes for electronic means as well as what platforms need to take into account.

Context and Principles

Let's cover the context and principles of the art of art that can be considered ADR. Unironic means that is negotiating, mediating or arbitrating through the internet. However, there are certain principles such as accountability or transparency, which we must uphold, because otherwise an electronic platform using OCR is not trustworthy. Let's take a look. We are talking about finding efficient approaches for dispute resolution. So historically, the first move towards efficiency was ADR as an alternative to litigation, negotiation, mediation and arbitration methods that are faster, more efficient and less costly than courts then claim or they are, is the next step and even more flexible in a way costly approach to dispute resolution.

Doing so could simply o.d are also known as ADR or alternative IVR or virtual IVR is a broad term that encompasses many forms of ADR and even litigation itself by incorporating electronic means into the dispute resolution process, including the use of internet, email, streaming video and other IP tools. When using ADR, both parties may not even need to meet face to face in May to communicate solely through the internet. All three main forms of IVR have electronic versions, so negotiation exists in any negotiation or electronic negotiation or cyber negotiation, which may be automated or assisted in automated negotiation. Both parties submit monetary figures to an algorithm that compares them with the average for similar situations and then outputs a settlement suggestion.

In the system negotiation, the parties simply negotiate over the Internet using emails or web video or others as proof of the communication. In terms of mediation, electronic mediation simply involves a neutral third party mediating the settlement, but using the Internet for its processes and evaluation. Electronic arbitration involves the third party making a binding decision, but again over the Internet. After hearing arguments and seeing the evidence online with documents, submissions, streaming, video teleconferencing or others. OCR is mostly used nowadays by specific websites or corporations to signal people that they are safe in case something goes wrong.

For example, eBay has an audio platform and the goal is for any person to know that if a dispute arises, eBay's or the platform can deal with it effectively and generate results for you. Usually, the art sounds relies on six principles that must be obeyed for successful implementation. The first is accountability. In short, providing effective results in terms of resolution that external parties can recognize as valid. The second is transparency. Every party involved should have transparency on redress options, decisions, as well as the costs and iterations of all processes involved.

In many cases, there is a tradeoff here with confidentiality, because the more confidential information is the waste and vice versa. The third principle is accessibility. In other words, users should have access to their information constantly at any time of the day. Any time you say. Naturally, Of course. Can't you? Downtime on the platform. But otherwise everything must be accessible. After that, credibility or accreditation. In short, the

ADR processes in ADR should be built on a foundation of quality. The professionals should be accredited by associations or by other means. Then comes security. The platform must store confidential information in verifying identities. Again, sometimes there is a trade off here with transparency.

The more transparent that the platform is showing results to the outside world, the less secure and confidential information is and vice versa. And finally, enforceability. In short order, your decisions must be legally enforceable. Something worth mentioning also comes up frequently in ADR procedures and actually in all ADR procedures is the matter of choice of law. Or in other words, when both parties are in different territories. Which law governs the dispute. The rule of thumb in the air is that if both parties belong to different nations, they usually agree on a jurisdiction together. And in case of lack of agreement, the one selected is the one for the audio provider's location.

So if someone in the UK and someone in Germany have a dispute using a platform headquartered in the United States, if they cannot agree on a jurisdiction, it's the United States law. If this is not possible, when the partners usually choose one of the main conventions or more the laws for international dispute resolution. So, Charles, for example, the United Nations Commission on International Trade, the laws more the law on e-commerce or the UN Convention on the use of electronic communications of international contracts, or the New York Convention, which helps foreign arbitration be recognized worldwide? What are some examples of the context and principles of who they are? The first are settlements and the words we touched on this previously.

How are all your decisions enforceable in order to be enforceable? These decisions usually come in settlement agreements, which are contracts that must be enforced by a court later, or arbitral awards which are binding, but only if all parties agree to them. Then comes transparency versus confidentiality is mentioned. There is a tradeoff here. On one hand, details must be kept confidential. But on the other hand, transparency helps show results in trust in your platform. And finally, there are different shapes for the audience. There are specific other mechanisms for negotiation. Settlements. Mediation in many other forms. As long as the dispute resolution is achieved through digital means. What are our key takeaways here? The first is that, oh, this is simply electronic ADR.

It's an open framework for ADR, for digital means which further reduces costs and increases flexibility. Even litigation, which is not a form of ADR itself, can also be augmented by VR by making it electronic. Out of curiosity, these are known as cyber courts versus traditional courts. Then all forms of ADR exist in ADR. There are implementations of negotiation, mediation and arbitration processes, and there are usually one or multiple versions of or the are for each. And finally, there are six principles for ADR to be successful. There must be accountability so that decision can be enforced.

There must be transparency in terms of data accessibility to that data. Credibility in the processes used. Security of data and identities and enforceability of the decisions. So as we see over the arc of ADR, electronic means and other types of ADR are also available in the art. However, there are certain principles that we must uphold, such as transparency or accountability, because the platform is not going to be trustworthy if we can't access our data. If the decision is non enforceable or other problems.

Steps and Categories

Let's cover the steps of an auditor too, as well as the categories of these. There is usually a fixed set of steps that both parties can go through in order to. And there is not just one type of ADR tool, but several for specific purposes. And we are going to cover both. Although there may be specific stamps for specific types of ADR in only our process is usually composed of three main steps. In the first step, the decision support algorithm provides feedback on the likely outcomes in amounts for negotiation for both parties. Then in the second step, both parties attempt to resolve any conflict among themselves by communicating directly through the ADR to negotiation.

Then, in the third step, if the issue is not resolved with negotiation and both parties return to the decision support algorithm to present different amounts or suggest tradeoffs in order to resolve the dispute. If this result is not acceptable, then the tool allows both parties to return to the previous step recursively where they communicate among themselves and repeat the process until resolution. Essentially, it's the same as an off line ADR negotiation process, but with a decision support tool. Although most of the tools follow this process, they can usually be categorized into three major times.

The first are electronic ADR tools. These are tools that are used to replicate ADR approaches in this type of environment. So for example, negotiation, mediation and arbitration, using digital means for efficiency and for evidence, as we've seen when cyber courts, these are courts that use digital means for more effective litigation. In this case, it's not ADR, it's the litigation, but few online means, but also possibly for court based EPR. These are still ADR procedures such as arbitration, but the third party involved is a court instead of just an expert in. Finally, there are internal ADR tools, for example, an internal merchant tool where consumers can present disputes.

This is usually something internal and it's a value add to the client of a retailer or platform. What are some examples of the steps in categories are the first are cyber courts. As mentioned, they are a parallel example. Instead of OCR being used for an ADR procedure, it's or are used for litigation cyber courts in being more agile and more flexible than traditional courts. They allow for the structured communication, the data, testimony and decisions. The second example is blind bidding. It's an example of an electronic negotiation tool. In this type of tool, both sides submit proposals without knowing what the other side proposes so blindly in.

Usually, if they are both within 30% of each other, the difference is split among both and the dispute is resolved. Finally, choosing the right tool is important. Even with OCR. By this I mean if one party, for example, has more power than a negotiation in the other one, the fact that the negotiation is electronic is not going to fix that. What are our key takeaways here? The first is that there are three main steps to any or the R tool. The parties need to know more about the likely outcomes, namely communicate and try to negotiate, and if necessary, they go back and rework those offers.

Second, there are three main categories: two audio tools that can be split into electronic ADR, which is simply ADR via the Internet and cyber courts, which are just for litigation over the Internet and internal AVR tools, which have the purpose of a retailer or merchant dealing with their clients. Each one of these is tailored for specific use cases, and finally VR is still in the air. So all challenges of it for me, for example, if mediation won't count in arbitration is necessary, then regardless of using possibly the best electronic mediation in the world, that problem will still remain.

So. As we see, there are different categories of audio tools for different purposes, such as cyber courts, internally, VR and more. And there is also a fixed set of steps in another process. But remember, at the end of the day, whatever doesn't work with ADR is not going to work now just because it's electronic. For example, if negotiation doesn't work because both. Parties can't come to a consensus. They're not going to come to a consensus just because they're now using an electronic platform. So all the challenges of ADR still remain.

Implementation and Case Studies

Let's talk about implementations and case studies. So far we've been talking about the theoretical part of ABR, for example, negotiation using animatronic platforms. But if you ask how do we do it in specific or how has it been done in the real world? That's exactly what we're going to cover with these case studies. It's covered ADR through OCR results in specific implementations for negotiation, mediation or arbitration. They're simply done online. So usually cyber negotiation or electronic negotiation platforms allow for multi-party negotiation, including negotiations with single or multiple clauses. The specific example is our blind bidding tools. In these tools, both parties submit offers blind to what the other side is offering.

So usually if these offers are within the margin of each other, such as 30%, they are automatically accepted and the difference is split between both parties. Then cyber mediation in these disputes communicate with a mediator or mediators who e-mail, videoconference or other online needs, and all evidence is recorded in an AI system. And finally, cyber arbitration. Here, the disputes register on the platform. We enter dispute information fee arbitration fees, and then an algorithm automatically determines the time and the number of arbitrators to use based on the information provided. An interesting case study and we can take a look at is the AI can, in my view, use the collaboration for domain name disputes where the IPO is.

The World Intellectual Property Organization in the IRP is the uniform domain name dispute resolution policy. So this is a collaboration resulting in the universal dispute resolution platform for domain name disputes in the languages, the WIPO for credibility. And it's also transparent because any decision making the platform is immediately available in text with a high level of detail. This procedure is also compulsory, so the DRP or the uniform domain name resolution policy is imposed on all registrants, no exception in regardless of which the main name provider they use. It's also self-executing. So cases are always closed two months after filing, and foreign authorities cannot intervene after a decision has been made.

It also benefits from the fact that the matter of the main names has public interest, which attracts the press and promotes accountability for decisions and the process of profits. All interaction is electronic, which forces the use of OCR, resulting in high speed and efficiency in the process. Even if the students want to communicate without electronic means, they just can't. So in this case, we see how two renowned institutions with a standardized process that is mandatory for everyone have created the solution to reduce cross-border, self-contained and to be transparent. Another interesting case study is one of the collaboration between the Asian or American Arbitration Association and Cyber Cell, which is a strategic alliance benefiting the kinds of both cyber for negotiation and the aim for mediation or arbitration.

So in short, clients can use cyber cells to negotiate. If we solve the dispute, perfect. But if they can't, then they can resort to the agent to mediate or even arbitrate the dispute. The main benefits of this collaboration include first leveraging the reputation of both. The EU is a non-profit which focuses on educating arbitrators, hosting publications and fostering the industry. Cyber Settle is an established EE negotiation provider and a pioneer in the space. Then there's experience in regulation. For example, the aim is commercial arbitration in mediation procedures. For many cases that are established and have been used by lawyers, arbitrators in many high value cases in both platforms themselves have handled hundreds of thousands of transactions.

In this case, we see how using incredible institutions leads to the creation of a unified solution. That is flexible and provides multiple services for the students. What are some examples of implementations and case studies of AVR? The first is that it's all about efficiency. What most successful audio tools in these studies have in common is that disputes can efficiently resolve the issue, which is their main goal. Then they are equal to all four retailers or merchants implementing all the procedures. The highest success levels are reached when the process is either available to all or mandatory to all standardize.

And finally, there are multiple elements that reinforce the choice of a platform by users, and none of them is better than the others that have incredible institutions, transparency, public accountability, and others all count here. What key takeaways do we have for this chapter? The first is that all ADR processes and even litigation, which is not AVR, can all be implemented for OCR. This results in very specific implementations which serve very specific purposes. The second reason is that I can wipe your case study. Their collaboration shows success due to elements such as credibility, poll transparency on results, and, above all else, efficiency.

And the third is the reasons why the case study of unique insight is successful. They provide an earlier platform than two averages. Their experience offers a range of services and has established proven procedures and again, is efficient. So as we see, although we've been talking about in general using mediation for the Internet or using arbitration for electronic means, when you implement these, these become very specific instances. And as we saw in the case studies, there are many precautions that you need to take in order for your platform to be trustworthy at the end of the day.

End Of The OCR

We are now at the end of the OCR chapter. Let's take a moment just to cover the different topics that we've covered related to online dispute resolution, as well as consolidate our knowledge with some questions. With this, we closed the online dispute resolution chapter where we covered the context and implementations of OCR. To achieve this, we explored three key topics in terms of online dispute resolution. The first was covering both the context and principles of audio, how it came about, and what it represents. Then we covered the different steps and categories of OCR. What are the usual steps in an overall process as well as the different categories of OCR tools? And finally, we covered the different implementations in case studies of all the tools for specific purposes.

Some questions that you can ask yourself to consolidate the knowledge in this chapter include. First, what are some of the six OCR principles? Which one in specific does this transparency usually clash with? Besides, in your litigation itself can also be then put online dispute resolution. What is the name given to this implementation? What are the two types of electronic negotiation or cyber negotiation? What are they consistent with? Why is OCR used by many merchants or retailers? What are the three major categories of IVR tools? Are these three what our internal ADR tools mostly used for? And lastly, Holden's choice of law occurs for OCR procedures. With this, we close the OCR chapter where we try to cover how to solve disputes through electronic means.

Dispute Resolution In The Merchant Banking

We are now at a dispute resolution in the merchant banking chapter. In this chapter we are going to cover how to help you merchants solve disputes or what is the process if you are a merchant bank, also known as an acquiring bank. Let's take a moment to cover the topics and goals for this chapter. Hi and welcome to the chapter about disputes in merchant banking. In this chapter we will cover dealing with dispute resolution that involves client merchants as a merchant or acquiring bank. Let's take a look at where we are. Before diving into the chapter, first we cover alternative dispute resolution approaches negotiation, mediation, arbitration and implementations of deals.

Then we covered the OCR or online dispute resolution framework. We cover that within our framework, its context, and how it's implemented. Now we are at the merchant banking chapter. We are going to cover how merchant banks deal with disputes, what type of processes they have and how they optimize this operation. And finally, we will cover specific chargeback reason codes. What types of reasons chargebacks usually have are divided into fraud, authorization errors, processing errors, and consumer disputes as well as recommendations for every type of reason. Code. What are our goals in this chapter? Our major one is to cover how to deal with dispute resolution as a merchant bank.

It's the major one. But more in specific, we will cover first the different types of disputes that may occur for different payment systems. Then general guidelines, including efficient trial use of lean digital systems, among others, to make this process more optimized. Then what is the lifecycle of a dispute as well as the different components of each? And finally, what dictates the involvement of the payment scheme as well as its consequences on the dispute resolution process. We are going to cover four main topics in terms of dispute resolution for merchant banks. The first are the general guidelines, general tips on how merchant banks can better deal with dispute resolution to satisfy their merchant clients than disputes by payment system clarifying what are debit credit issue prepaid and ATM disputes and fraud in specific in how they are performed.

Then we'll cover the dispute lifecycle. What happens when a dispute is raised usually by the issuing bank as a chargeback and how both banks are involved in this process? And finally, we'll cover scheme involvement in which situations the payment scheme becomes officially involved in a dispute and the consequences of that involvement. So as you see in this chapter, we are going to cover everything about dispute resolution for banks related to their merchant clients, the process, the types of disputes and more.

General Guidelines

Let's talk about some general guidelines to resolve disputes as a merchant bank. That is, what do the best things do in terms of supporting their merchant clients, in terms of disputes? Or if you already do it, how can you do it even better? That's what we're going to cover. There are multiple ways in which merchant or acquiring banks can improve their operations. The first is by streamlining and reducing information silos. This means having less dispute resolution centers, for example, for big institutions that cover a lot of geographical areas, which in turn causes less weight for their merchant clients. Also, using digital lead platforms helps because it allows for easy document offload and tracking of disputes. It allows for open dispute resolution.

The second way to improve operations is through better classification and triage. This can be done by easily classifying the different types of disputes, usually by payment system, automated clearinghouse, prepaid credit, debit ATM or others. Also, using simple rules for triage also helps, for example, never resolving low value disputes such as below \$50 because the cost is just not worth it. Focusing on dispute resolution results is also important here. That is, trying to ensure results for merchant clients instead of just regulatory compliance. In many cases, institutions just want to follow the rules and don't really focus on helping the merchants, which erodes customer loyalty. It's also important to enforce accountability. Specifically having owners with resolution kickbacks.

These practices are important because they affect relationships with merchant clients. Many institutions focus just on the process and obeying regulations, missing important opportunities to gain customer trust by helping their customers obtain results in disputes. Additionally, the use of lean digital processes, especially when coupled with artificial intelligence, can lead institutions to learn more about patterns in dispute resolution, such as which types of disputes are easily resolved, among other things, which can accelerate triage and resolution of disputes resulting in a positive feedback loop. What are some examples of general guidelines for dispute management? The first are digital platforms.

The use of lean and secure digital platforms for document submission can easily accelerate dispute resolution, mediation and arbitration for all involved parties. Second, having less dispute resolution centers, reducing the number of VR centers, for example, by region helps streamline operations and also standardizes the processes used in finally focusing on quality. Although many banks only care about obeying regulations, helping merchant clients helps ensure their trust and reduces attrition risk of losing them to competitors. What are our key takeaways here? The first is that dispute resolution should be mean and efficient. One way to increase efficiency is to break down silos and streamline processes, resulting in last week's time for clients.

The adoption of simple classification mechanisms can easily root disputes internally, while triage can help not waste time with cases that are just not worth it. In finally focusing on results, merchants know when they're being helped and when they're not, and this is reflective in customer trust and long term relationships. So as we see, there are many ways to create a better service for merchants. To resolve disputes, you can be more lean and efficient. You can have a triage system where disputes are more efficient. But at the end of the day, the merchant has to feel like you are helping them with the process. Because if you're not helping them and they're a client, you're not going to be a client for very long.

Disputes by Payment System

But let's talk about the dispute lifecycle. That is usually when you have a dispute in terms of two banks, there is what is called a formal chargeback process. It is the issuing bank. The bank of the credit card involved in the dispute requests the acquiring bank to return the money from that transaction. Let's take a look at the process in specific. One of the most efficient tenets of efficient dispute resolution for any bank is properly separating the different types of disputes. Usually this is done by payment system. So you have credit card disputes, debit card disputes, exchange disputes, prepay disputes and disputes. There are different nuances among them. So it's important to note the differences.

Debit and credit card disputes are similar, and they have to do with a disagreement between a merchant Andy card holder. Usually over a specific transaction or a specific product. While credit card disputes involve cardholder credit and therefore the fact that the issuing bank creates credit risk for them. Debit card disputes involve funds that are already owned by an account owner, which causes damage to the money. And surprisingly, banks tend to intervene in credit disputes much more often than in debit once. This type of dispute can be caused by actual crops. For example, someone may steal a card number or impersonate a person or make false claims about a product to obtain a refund or others.

Naturally, it may also be caused by reasons that are not real, such as a processing error or a consumer dispute about goods delivered. AC Disputes have to do with the automated clearing house system in the United States. This is a system. It processes transactions. They are awaiting clearance for their destination, as the name says. Frequently, the cause of this type of dispute is from. So someone modifies the AC files to change transaction amounts or set new recipients that were not originally included to receive money. Or someone can actually steal money from an account until the transaction is processed, taking advantage of that time. Whack. Prepay disputes have to do with these agreements over the usage of prepaid cards, and these are frequently due to fraud.

So a fraudster can go into a store and exchange a fake card with a real one, or they can trick clerks into giving them the pins to these cards so that they can withdraw money, usually pretending to be a member of the security team or actually SIM cards actually replicating the magnetic strip. Or just use stolen cards. Finally, ATM disputes have to do with these agreements over amounts obtained from ATMs. Some of these disputes are classified as consumer disputes. For example, when the consumer argues that they did not receive the full transaction value due to a faulty ATM, even if it is machine error, it's still considered a consumer dispute. Further disputes are naturally due to fraud.

So a fraudster may use simple or complex methods for fraud, ranging from placing a warning sign such as a piece of paper over the cash receptacle so that people think that it's out of order. And then the fraudster just takes the piece of paper out and withdraws the money, or using devices to skim cards in, copy their information in cameras to record people inputting the pins, or they can replicate a full ATM machine with a fake one that seems like it's not working and just collects codes or even ripping a full ATM off the wall to load onto a truck. What are some examples of disputes by payment system? The first area is credit and debit disputes. While card fraud in general affects a lot of people, credit fraud usually has higher priority. This is because it's a credit risk for the issuing bank. The money is on credit while with added fraud.

It isn't because only the account owner's money is affected. Prepaid fraud is a type of fraud that hurts merchants deeply because there is no specific issuing bank for prepaid cards. The merchant doesn't have a lot of reBook. Nobody to turn to in case things go wrong. And finally, there are many variations of ATM fraud and they are all dangerous. The fraudster working with cameras, devices, or even actual people stealing cards and recording pins. What are our key takeaways here? The first is that efficient triage matters. Knowing the different payment systems and the disputes within each is important in order to perform efficiently.

Four different department cards usually work the same. While there are multiple types of froth, card fraud usually involves common elements such as stealing card numbers, replicating the magnetic strip or similar. And finally, for all cases, disputes may represent fraud or not. There are cases where a dispute means fraud, but this is not always the case. So as we see, we usually have this process of retrieval request chargeback and second chargeback in fraud the way the acquiring bank can behave in different ways. Resolving to dispute or not in. In the last case scenario, if both banks just can't seem to get to an understanding, then the payment scheme itself can become involved and make a decision.

Dispute Life Cycle

But let's talk about the dispute lifecycle. That is usually when you have a dispute in terms of two banks. There is what is called a formal chargeback process. It is the issuing bank. The bank of the credit card involved in the dispute requests the acquiring bank to return the money from that transaction. Let's take a look at the process in specific. When a dispute occurs, a specific flow is triggered, which involves both the issuing bank representing the card holder of the card used in the purchase and the acquiring or merchant bank representing the merchant in the transaction. There are three possible stages in this process. By possible, I mean that they don't necessarily always occur, all of them.

But if they do occur, it's always in this order. The first step is what is called a retrieval request. So when a cardholder brings a dispute to an issuer bank before the charge backstage, which is where they demand the money back, this step may occur. It's before it. In this way, the issuer requests documentation from the merchant supporting a transaction through the acquiring bank. The acquiring bank may fulfill this request, which means replying to the request or not at all. After this we have the actual chargeback. A chargeback technically is the demand by an issuing bank to make good on a loss on a credit card. At this stage the acquirer may dispute the chargeback, sending documentation or just accept it.

If the dispute is not resolved during the first chargeback, then a second chargeback will occur. This is a new request by the issuing bank to make good on a loss, just like the first one. But in this case, it challenges the documents sent in the first one, and it may request more. Again, these may be sent or not. The existence of the second chargeback indicates that the first one was not resolved. Usually there are no chargebacks after the second. If the situation is not resolved here, then a mediation process usually occurs in the first stage. The retrieval request the issuer sends a request for documentation supporting a transaction. The acquirer bank may send the response or not, which is called fulfilling the request. If the acquirer sends that response, it may contain the documentation or not.

If it does contain it, it's considered a fulfillment. And if it's a response without documentation, it's considered in fulfillment. So you can have a non-response or you can have a response that may fulfill or not the retrieval request. This information usually includes the sales draft for the transaction in e-commerce or EMV transactions. The sales draft has usually already been sent by the system, but in case the merchant's legacy systems don't end with it, then what is called a substitute draft is generated and sent to the issuer. Naturally, this is in case the acquirer bank desires to fulfill the request. They may not. Usually, acquirer banks are in fact motivated to fulfill these requests because they want to avoid chargebacks.

So whenever an issuer sends a request to the acquirer, the bank usually quickly coordinates with the merchant to send the required information right away. The second step is the chargeback, which technically is a demand by the issuer to be reimbursed for their loss. This can take the format of a financial record to be settled or a case in a dispute management system.

The issuer usually provides what is called a reason code for the chargeback, which may represent fraud or an authorization error, a processing error or a consumer dispute. For this reason, code usually has this specific situation that generates the chargeback.

If the acquirer disagrees with a chargeback, they may explicitly acknowledge it or simply do nothing in a way of the transaction being settled in case they do accept it. Additionally, they may decide on whether to absorb the cost of the chargeback or force the merchant to absorb the costs themselves. If the acquirer bank does not agree with the chargeback, they can perform what is called a re presentment, also known as a second presentment of the information. In this case, they collect supporting documentation and the financial record of the transaction from the merchant and then they present it to the issuer bank. This may include the cardholder's signature evidence of shipment of goods or other supporting materials.

In some cases, if the issuer disagrees with the materials presented, if they're not good enough to dispute the chargeback, they can trigger a second. Chargeback. Just like the first one. It's for the man to make good on the cardholder's loss, and it usually states that the current documentation is not sufficient. If a second chargeback occurs in the issuer in acquirer banks still cannot agree. Then usually the payment scheme of their banking institution will arbitrate the dispute and make a decision themselves. This decision is usually in the form of the issuer bank being credited with the amount in the acquirer bank being debited with it. This is another reason why acquirer banks have the motivation to properly provide documentation in resolving chargeback disputes before it comes to this.

What are some examples of the dispute lifecycle? The first is the case of a valid chargeback. If a valid chargeback occurs, the acquiring bank may acknowledge it and settle the record or do nothing and let it be settled. Another example is the case of an invalid chargeback. If a chargeback is invalid, then the cardholder in the issuing bank representing them may drop the dispute after evidence is presented in the payment scheme. That is, the body that regulates the rules for banks may make a decision themselves. The payment scheme of the specific banking institutions involved usually has a set of predetermined rules to automatically resolve disputes in cases where both parties cannot agree.

What are our key takeaways here? The first is that this is usually a three step process. The dispute between a cardholder and merchant and their respective banks usually has three steps, the last of them being optional. They retrieval request the chargeback and the second chargeback documentation is crucial in this process. Most chargeback disputes are resolved based on the documentation, provided it's either convincing enough to resolve a dispute or the dispute remains. And finally, if the issuer and acquirer cannot agree in terms of the dispute, the payment scheme will be involved sooner or later.

They may start by mediating this situation, but in most cases they will end up actually arbitrating it. So as we see, we usually have this process of retrieval request chargeback and second chargeback in front, the way the acquiring bank can behave in different ways, resolving disputes or not. In the last case scenario, if both banks just can't seem to get to an understanding, then the payment scheme itself can become involved and make a decision.

Scheme Involvement

Let's talk about the possible involvement of the payment scheme that is the regulator or the association which defines the payment rules for that specific bank. So when two banks just can't seem to come to an understanding, this payment scheme can become involved. But they also have certain rules to allocate blame immediately without even beginning a dispute process. So let's take a look at some of these shortcuts. The usual three step process of retrieval request chargeback in second chargeback is usually long and complicated. So in order to facilitate dispute resolution, the payment schemes, that is, the bodies governing the processes of banking institutions have developed certain standards.

The first is the distinction between allocation and collaboration. In certain cases, the scheme may automatically allocate one side as responsible. So, for example, in one dispute this scheme, we take a look and allocate responsibility to the issuer bank, which has to drop the dispute if both parties agree with this allocation. This dispute is immediately resolved. It's a form of arbitration. But if they don't agree, they can resolve it among themselves, which is known as collaboration. So the scheme allocates responsibility in arbitrators' decisions. Or both parties collaborate. There's also usually free arbitration, and arbitration is at different stages.

What I mean is that the dispute can be sent to the scheme to analyze and to arbitrate. But before doing this, one bank may warn the other that they are moving towards arbitration.

That is called the pre arbitration stage and it serves as kind of a last warning in case they want to solve things without scheme involvement. And finally, there are liability shifts. These are rules. They meet with the nhai, a party there, to dispute rights. If they commit some fault or certain conditions are satisfied. For example, the most known one is the EMV liability shift. EMV chip technology is very secure and can detect fake cards. So if an EMV transaction is well performed, then no card issuer can ever dispute it, period.

The liability is on them. But on the other hand, if the merchant doesn't implement EMV technology the right way so they don't detect the card that is fake and that could have been detected, then the liability is shifted to that merchant and they cannot dispute a chargeback period. In terms of allocation, what happens is that the scheme proposes one party to be responsible and if both parties accept this, then the dispute is immediately resolved. In other words, an arbitration is suggested and if both parties don't accept that arbitration, they can mediate among themselves.

So if they don't accept that allocation, they resolve the dispute themselves. This usually happens through the usual three step process: retrieval request chargeback, second chargeback, and possibly mediation afterwards, which is a process known as collaboration between both parties. So both parties can either allocate or collaborate. Allocation is usually preferred for efficiency reasons because the payment scheme goes in with a specific time period, offers a specific settlement, and the dispute is resolved. Scheme arbitration usually occurs when both parties cannot reach a conclusion, so they turn to the scheme to analyze the case and present a solution, which is a type of mediation process itself.

And if the scheme solution is not accepted, both parties can request the scheme to arbitrate the dispute and make a binding decision. So in short, you have allocation, which is a fast arbitration, and if that doesn't happen, you have collaboration. Within that collaboration, both parties can ask the scheme to mediate the dispute, and if the mediation is not successful, they go back to arbitration. But a more complex one for cards is a bank may notify the other side that they are moving towards arbitration before doing it, giving them kind of a last chance to resolve things among themselves before this scheme is involved.

What are some examples of scheme involvement? The first is issuer allocation, the issue where a bank may raise a dispute claiming might of authorization, for example, but the merchant provides a signature. The scheme may allocate default to the issuer and resolve the dispute. Then collaboration. Both parties may have a dispute where the issuer doesn't accept the documents provided. But the acquirer insists on them so they don't accept the scheme allocation and they have to collaborate. And finally, the EMV liability shift, considering the security of an EMV transaction when one is properly processed, the new issuer can request a chargeback because the cardholder didn't make that purchase period.

But if an EMV transaction is wrongly done, then the issuer can and will demand the chargeback and it's the merchant's liability period. What are our key takeaways here? The first is allocation versus collaboration. The payment scheme may define specific rules that in certain situations automatically attribute fault to one party. Otherwise, both parties collaborate among themselves. Both parties may move to arbitration if they don't agree during collaboration. They may ask the scheme to mediate the dispute, and if the mediation resolution is still not accepted, they can ask the scheme to actually arbitrate the dispute. And finally, liability shifts occur.

The scheme usually contains rules that shift liability to certain parties, and there are certain conditions. For example, for successful EMV transactions, it's always the issuer's liability. They cannot deny that transaction. But for faulty EMV transactions, it's always the merchant's liability. The liability is shifted depending on the conditions and the liability shifts. Prevent a party from even disputing the transaction. So as we see, the payment scheme can become involved in actually arbitrate disputes and this can be requested by one of the banks. But they also came up with some heuristics, some shortcuts to even prevent these disputes from coming up in the first place. If they're easy to solve through allocation, through collaboration or for specific liability shifts.

What Next

And with this we reached the end of dispute resolution in the merchant banking chapter where we try to cover how to deal with disputes from your merchant clients. If you are a merchant bank or acquiring bank yourself, take a moment to recap our topics and consolidate our knowledge with some questions. We are now at the end of the merchant banking chapter where we covered how to deal with dispute resolution involving client merchants as their bank. To achieve this, we covered four main topics. The first were some general guidelines streamlining dispute resolution operations would better triage, better I.T. and other operational changes. The second was a distinction of the different dispute types by payment system, credit, debit exchange and others. Then we covered the dispute lifecycle, the three usual stages, as well as what the issuing and acquiring banks do at each stage.

And finally, we covered the situations in which the payment scheme becomes involved as well as what that entails. What are some questions that you can ask yourself to consolidate the knowledge of this chapter? What is the difference between allocation in collaboration in terms of disputes between issuer and acquirer banks? What are the usual three stages of a dispute process? Which ones are optional? What are the different payment systems? What is common about disputes or frauds involving cards? In which situations does the payment scheme become involved? What do they usually do? When does the second chargeback occur? What should acquirer banks do to provide better service to their merchant clients and boost loyalty? Can you think of a couple of ways with this? We closed the merchant banking chapter where we try to cover how to deal with disputes from your merchant clients. If you are a bank.

Chargeback Reason Codes

We are now at the chargeback reason codes chapter. In this chapter we are going to cover the reason codes embedded in chargebacks. This is when an issuing bank asks the acquiring bank to give back the money from a transaction. There's usually a specific reason code which symbolizes the reason for that chargeback. Let's take a moment to cover the topics from this chapter. Welcome to the Chargeback Reason Codes chapter. In this chapter we will shed light on the different types of reason codes for chargebacks requested by card holders and issuing banks. Where are we in terms of progress? We are now in the fourth chapter. For first we covered the different types of alternative dispute resolution negotiation, mediation, arbitration, specific implementations and hybrid approaches.

Then we covered online dispute resolution, its context, principles and implementation. After that, we covered how dispute resolution occurs in merchant banking general guidelines, the dispute lifecycle and scheme involvement. And now we are at the Chargeback Reason Codes chapter. We are going to explore the different reasons for Codes for Chargebacks by issuing banks. What are our goals in this chapter? The key one is to illustrate the different categories of recent codes by different card providers. Naturally, we cannot cover specific card companies or specific codes, but we will talk about the general categories and recommended actions more in detail.

We will cover first the different types of fraud from processing transactions with different amounts to EMV transactions to fact cards or merchants and others. Then there are the different types of consumer disputes ranging from disagreements over product quality or expectations to cancel transactions that we're still charged or they're not processing due credit. Also, authorization issues including the client non-existing or invalid authorization by the merchant. And finally, processing errors, including wrong codes, wrong locations, weight presentment, and other problems with the processing of the actual transaction. And before proceeding, I just want to mention a solution that a lot of my customers have been getting good experiences with, which is trivial payments.

And although I'm not formally associated with a company, I do like to recommend solutions here and there that make life easier for my payment professionals. So while a lot of the dispute resolution activities and functions that we are going to cover in the Book can be done from scratch. In reality, in most cases, they will be present in some sort of commercial solution. And this is good because it cuts on human resource costs and it reduces risk. Everything is in one place. So just to mention a lot of my clients, mainly in the UK but not always, have been talking to me about treble payments, which combines common fraud prevention and dispute resolution techniques in especially for card acquirers, including, for example, dashboards with real time sales refunds and other relevant analytics, or, for example, compliance with payment protocols such as 3D secure and also industry regulation such as the PCI assess. So this is a short and official mention of an example of a solution that a lot of my clients have been very happy with.

And if you're interested in them, we will link to them in the chapters and I'll also place it in the chapter description itself. In order to cover this topic, we will touch on the four main families of Reason Codes for Chargebacks. These include, first of all, from disputes raised due to suspicions of fraud both by the cardholder and the merchant. It includes five merchants, fraudulent transactions in others, then authorisation issues, merchants processing a transaction having been declined authorization, having invalid authorization information or just not having requested it in the first place. Then processing errors issues with the actual processing of the transaction, presenting a transaction to wait, using incorrect codes or incorrect transaction data.

And finally, consumer disputes are raised by consumers, including due to mismatches in expectations about the goods being charged for canceled or incomplete transactions and others. So as you see in this chapter, we are going to cover the broad categories of chargeback reason codes. We have four in total with many specific reason codes within each.

Fraud: Introduction

Let's talk about fraud. The reason: Coats. As the name says, this group of topics include situations where fraud actually occurred. There is some detail in the transaction that was actively misrepresented in order to charge the person without authorization using a stolen car charging the wrong amount in many other types. What's the component to cover this from is naturally one of the types of disputes that generate chargebacks. While most of these codes deal with merchant fraud, which causes the cardholder to request a chargeback, there are also cases where the card itself or the consumer is fraudulent, which makes their issuing bank detect it in request or chargeback as well.

We will cover different types of fraud. There are related to payments to unauthorized transactions, to transactions with different values than expected, as well as fraud due to the misuse or lack of use of EMV technology. We are going to tackle the reason codes for four types of fraud that generate chargebacks. The first are not authorized or recognized transactions. These are reason codes related to transactions that the cardholder does not think that they authorized or does just not remember. The second or flag or monitor merchants or cards. These are chargebacks due to the merchant or the card being identified as fraudulent and being present in what's called the hotlist that identifies known offenders.

Then fraudulent processing, which is the name given to a situation where a transaction is processed with a different value than what was authorized or multiple charges are made that were not authorized in finally the EMV liability shift chargebacks that occur due to fraud that occurred when EMV technology could have prevented it but didn't because the merchant didn't know how to use it or did not use it well. This is a merchant's liability. So as you see in this group of four topics, we are going to cover reason codes where fraud actually occurred.

Fraud: Not Authorized/Recognised

Let's talk about not authorized or not recognizing transactions. As the name says. This kind of reason code occurs when the person looks at their bank balance and they think, Oh, I don't recognize this transaction. It can be legitimate or not. It is. The merchant may have actually charged the person without authorization or the person may have authorized it, but they just don't remember. So let's take a look at this type of reason code in specific. This specific reason code is provided when the cardholder believes that there is potential fraud because either they don't recognize a transaction or they believe they have not authorized it.

Naturally, this almost always occurs in card, not present transactions, usually in e-commerce, because people can easily identify transactions in which they have used their card physically. There are exceptions though, but mostly this reason code indicates transactions where the card was not present. It's important to notice that disputes with this reason code may be valid or not because the consumer may have authorized the transaction that merely has a different merchant name or description from what they fought, which is frequent when the merchant's brand name is not their legal name and their legal name is what appears on the transaction.

But it can also be valid. In the case of actual fraud in this type of dispute, the merchants usually simply need to provide proof that the transaction was actually authorized by the cardholder. If the card company provides device address verification services for this card, it's also recommended for the merchant to show proof that they obtained a positive match and shipped the goods to that location. In short, proof that they really sent the goods to the consumer. And if it's the case, the merchant should also provide the proof that the chargeback is invalid because it doesn't adhere to card issuer requirements.

For example, if the consumer states this too late or tries to contest an EMV chip transaction or possibly proof that the cardholder no longer wishes to dispute the transaction or any other specific situation that may be the case. What are some examples of non authorized or non recognized transactions? The first is having an unauthorized expense. A cardholder sees a 3799 transaction on the card and they know that they haven't authorized it. So there is a dispute. The second is having a valid, yet forgotten transaction. A cardholder sees a $200 charge in the contest because they don't recognize it. But later they do recognize it. They remember the purchase and they drop the dispute.

Another example is having a transaction that is from a known merchant, but the transaction itself is unknown. For example, the cardholder sees a transaction for 179 that is from a known merchant and is similar to past purchases, but they don't remember authorizing this specific one. What are our key takeaways here? The first is that this type of reason code simply represents a situation where the cardholder does not recognize the specific transaction or did not authorize it. It can be valid or invalid. It may represent true fraud or not. It can be raised because an unauthorized transaction was charged, but it may also be valid and just forgotten to the user.

And finally, the merchant usually only has to show proof of authorization, since the code is about the transaction not being authorized or recognized. The merchant only has to show proof that the transaction was in fact authorized. Very simple. So as we see this type of reason, code is raised when the transaction was not authorized or is not recognized if it can be valid or not. But usually there is no way to contest it except to show active proof that the transaction was in fact authorized.

Fraud: Fraudulent Processing

Let's talk about fraudulent processing. Reason codes. This usually occurs when a merchant is sort of charging one transaction charge, multiple ones, and usually with the same authorization. For example, you buy a flat screen for $500, but instead of being charged $500, once you are charged $500, three or four times within the same five minute limit. Let's take a look at how this occurs in specific. The chargeback reason code indicating fraudulent processing indicates that any transaction was authorized by the cardholder, but it was not the one that actually occurred. It was a different value or additional transactions were performed that were not authorized.

In other words, the processing of the transaction itself was fraudulent. Therefore, the name. This is a code that frequently comes up when a merchant has authorization for one transaction but performs multiple ones within a short period of time, such as 5 to 10 minutes. These can be duplicates of the original transaction or other transactions with different values upon receiving a chargeback with this type of reason code. A merchant should provide documentation that proves, among other things, that consumer authorization was provided for all transactions performed, that all of these transactions performed are separate, and that each one in of itself is a legitimate transaction, not a duplicate. If it's the case also proof that the additional transactions were already credited to the cardholder if it's the case.

So if the merchant admits the mistake, they have to show proof that they have already credited the value back. Or if it's the case, proof that the cardholder doesn't wish to dispute the transactions anymore. What are some examples of fraudulent processing? The first is a triple charge. Maybe a consumer purchases a product for 1799, but they realize that they were charged three times that amount by the merchant as three separate transactions. Another example are their charges. The consumer buys a product for $200, but they realize that there are other multiple charges with random values, such as $1 or $15 all within minutes.

And the third example is additional services, the cardholder purchases, a service that includes a $500 product. And there are several small fees of $10, 15 or other that may be charged as part of the contract. But the cardholder considers that only the $500 purchase was valid and that the other fees are not part of the contract. What are our key takeaways here? The first is that fraudulent processing represents a dispute where the merchant will have authorization for a transaction, but they perform a different one or multiple ones in succession. There is a strict time period for this type of situation because the additional transactions are usually performed with the same authorization for the initial one, which has an expiry date.

So there is usually a short time period for this between 5 to 15 minutes where all transactions occur. And finally, the merchant should address this type of situation by providing transaction documents that prove that each transaction is legitimate, unique and authorized. So as we see fraudulent processing is fraud related to the processing of the transaction itself. And in fact, processing it more times than should have occurred in the only way to fight this type of reasoned code is to show by the merchant that they had specific authorization for a charge that occurred.

Fraud: Monitored Merchant or Card

Let's talk about monitored merchants or cards. These are two types of reason codes, but they kind of symbolize the same thing. Monitors cards are cards which are recognized to be criminal or associated with fraud, while monitored merchants are the same. But on the merchant side it is. This merchant was flagged for performing fraud or at least something fishy. Let's take a look at these two types of differences. But related. Reason codes to parallel. Yet similar situations occur when either the card used for a transaction or the merchant on the other side of that transaction are flagged by the monitoring program or initiative of a card association. In other words, they are what is called hot waste. They are part of the list that identifies known offenders.

So Visa, MasterCard and other card associations have hot lists of fraudulent merchants and cards that are usually two distinct mechanisms one for each. So if the card used or the merchant involved are hacker listed, a reason code will be used to fight this. Again, usually there will be two distinct reason codes for a fight merchant or card. Although fraudulent transactions with five merchants or five cards may fall into other categories, such as unrecognized transactions. This type of reason code is used when no other code is provided. In other words, if you have a flight of a merchant accused of an unrecognized transaction, then the reason code will be an unrecognized transaction. But if you just have a flagged merchant in no other issue, then the reason code will be flagged merchant.

And the same for the cards. In both cases where the credit card or the merchant are flagged, fraud review cases will be opened usually in the respective bank. So the issuing bank for the cardholder, if the card is still in the acquiring or merchant bank of the merchant, if they are the ones where situations involving this reason, however, can be minimized by maintaining accurate records. In the case of both banks, granular and transparent data helps feed fraud monitoring solutions and find both fraudulent cards in fraudulent merchants faster. And in many cases, it even prevents fraud. What are some examples of monitored merchants or monitoring cards? Very simple. The first is an example of a flagged card.

If the credit card used was flagged by Hotlist in New, the recent code is provided for the transaction. The merchant will receive a chargeback request claiming that the credit card was flagged and is fraudulent. And the opposite is a fake merchant. If the merchant themselves have been performing fraudulent activity, then the bank of the cardholder may issue a reason code if there is no other reason code indicating that the merchant is flagged. What are our key takeaways here? The first is that this type of reason code indicates that a flag, merchant or card were involved. These are usually two distinct mechanisms in two distinct codes. But the principle is the same.

Either the merchant or the card have been flagged as fraudulent in the hotlist. The second is that when a merchant or a cardholder are identified as flagged, then a fraud case will be opened with their banks. In the case of the merchant, it's the merchant or acquirer bank. In the case of the card, it's the card's issuing bank. And finally, this specific reason code is used when there are no other explicit reasons. So if the merchant is fraudulent and involved in fraudulent processing, which is a reason code by itself, then the fraudulent processing reason code will be the one used and so on.

This code is usually only used if other codes are not if there are no other reasons besides this. So as we see, these are two types of reason codes which are different but work in exactly the same manner. Either the card itself was flagged as being associated with crime or fraud, or the merchant themselves, on the other hand, is associated with fraud, war, crime. But the reason codes work in exactly the same manner.

Fraud: EMV Liability Shift

Let's talk about the EMV liability shift in specific from the card company to the merchant. What this means is a fog. It can be simplified as EMV technology can detect almost any type of card fraud. So if a merchant has EMV technology but fraud occurs anyway, then it's their fault not the card companies. It can be summarized as you have all the technology possible to prevent fraud. So if you did not prevent fraud and it occurred, you only have yourself to blame. Let's take a look at this recent code in specific. The chargeback reason relating to the EMV liability shift has to do with allocating fault to a merchant that did not properly finish an EMV transaction. In order to understand this chargeback reason. We have to first understand what the EMV liability shift is.

So in the past, card companies like Visa and MasterCard were liable for fraud. That was performed with cards when they had no chips and just magnetic strips. As you can guess, this caused heavy losses for them. So this led to them developing new technology in the form of EMV chips. These provide a stronger level of authentication in which EMV devices can detect fake cards. So these were soon rolled out and represent most cards in the world today. So what happened was the card companies stated that any fraud that occurs due to not leveraging these EMV chips or incorrectly using them is the business's fault. It's the merchants fault and not the card companies. Therefore, it's a liability shift.

The liability is the merchants and not the card companies. In other words, the card companies pretty much said, Hey, we developed the perfect technology to the tech trough. So if you don't use it correctly, you are the one who is liable for that fraud, not us. So naturally, this code occurs when a fake card is used by the cardholder. And it could be detected by EMV chip technology. But it's not detected because the merchant either didn't leverage an EMV chip reader to detect the fake card, or they used a chip either, but wrongly. So in short, the merchant did not know how to use EMV technology and they did not prevent fraud that they could have prevented if they had just used the right tools the right way.

Usually there are one or more circumstances. It must occur in this type of situation. The first possibility is that the merchant did not use a chip reading device for the transaction. They read the magnetic strip. In other words, if they had the rather chip because they attacked a fake card, but because they didn't, they didn't detect it. The second is that the merchant used a chip reading device, but it was not an EMV pin compliant one. In other words, they probably used a cheaper device that could not detect fake cards. They used technology, but they did not use EMV technology. It's still a problem.

And the third possibility is that the transaction was a CHIP initiative and possibly with a valid PIN, but the PIN information was not transmitted in the authorization request. In other words, even if they did obtain EMV authorization, if it did not make its way to the merchant's records, it's exactly the same as never having had it. Additionally, there are some reason codes that make the distinction between counterfeit cards and non counterfeit cards in EMV transactions. So for the case of a counterfeit card, it's what we mentioned. The cardholder claims that a fake card was used or their stolen card and the merchant did not properly identify it because they didn't use a chip operation.

But in the case of a non-qualified card, the card holder claims that the card used was real but chip technology was not used or it was non EMV compliant in fraud was performed anyway. In both cases, unless the merchant provides documentation to the contrary. So documentation that they did complete a proper EMV transaction. It's always their liability due to the lack of use or misuse of EMV technology. But this distinction remains. What are some examples of EMV liability shift situations? The first is when the merchant doesn't ask for the chip pin, they use the card with a magnetic strip either. So a counterfeit card will not be detected, but it would be detected if it were a chip operation.

The second is using non-compliant technology. Some merchants use chip readers that are not EMV compliant. For example, Because they're cheaper. So they do read the chip in me, ask for a pen, but they don't properly process EMV transactions, so they may not detect fraud in the merchant. Yes. What is still responsible? Finally, incomplete authentication is another example. Maybe there is an online transaction. Little averages and chip reader that starts with the machine and then continues. Even if the correct pin is rare and it's EMV compliant if it's not transmitted to the online portion, there is no record of the authentication.

In this case, it's still considered an EMV liability by the merchant. If the information is not stored, it's the same as never having to have it. What are our key takeaways here? The first is the EMV liability shift. This is a shift in liability from card companies to merchants. After EMV technology was rolled out. In short, card companies give merchants all the necessary technology to detect fraud. So if they don't use that technology, well, it's their liability, not the card companies. This can occur for multiple reasons, not having a proper device, not asking for the pin or others in both situations. A fake card is not detected and it's the merchant's liability.

And finally, there can be cases of incomplete authentication, maybe a valid EMV pin was processed but is not transmitted maybe due to a technology or integration issue. And in that case, it's the same as information never having arrived, and it's therefore still the merchant's liability. So as we see the EMV liability shift within code can be summarized as as a merchant, you had the perfect technology to prevent fraud. So if you didn't do it, then the fault is automatically yours. And it usually occurs when the merchant uses a machine which is not EMV compliant or when they don't use the machine at all.

Authorization: Introduction

Let's talk about authorization reason codes. This group of topics cover situations where the transaction was not authorized or authorization was not requested in the first place. Let's take a look at this in more detail. Reason Codes that have to do with authorization reasons are usually due to incomplete or missing authorization for a transaction on part of the merchant. There are a myriad of reasons for this. It can be as simple as authorization never having been requested in the first place or having been the client. But there can be more subtle and complex situations such as authorizations that were requested for a different incorrect account number or for different transaction amounts or authorization with invalid information having been communicated. We are going to explore three key types of authorization reason codes. The first is missing or declined authorization.

Very simple. Either the merchant was declined authorization or they're not even asked for it in the first place. But they still process the transaction. The second reason codes related to lost or stolen cards or cards there are marked as in recovery by the card company. Naturally, because the card is not being held by the cardholder, any authorization with it cannot be authorized in final transactions within valid information authorization information that includes invalid or incomplete information. So as we see this type of reason, code symbolizes transactions where authorization was not obtained, it was the claim or it was not requested in the first place, but also a couple of other specific scenarios.

Authorization: Missing/Declined Authorization

Let's talk about missing or the client authorization. This reason code is raised for when the merchant is not authorized to charge a certain amount or when they did not request authorization in the first place. The simplest way to think about this is when you place your card into a post and it says declined. But there are other specific situations. For example, you charge the value with a tip, but you only obtain authorization to charge the value without the tip. So technically, you don't have authorization for that specific value whatsoever. These scenarios, this type of reason code usually indicates one of two specific situations, both related to not having authorization for a transaction. The first is that the merchant did request authorization for a transaction, but it was the client and the transaction was processed anyway.

The second type is that the merchant made no attempt whatsoever to obtain authorization for the transaction, or they made an attempt after the fact and the transaction again was processed anyway. Both situations result in the merchant having processed a transaction that they have no authorization for either because it was declined or just missing. There are multiple measures that can be taken by merchants in order to avoid this type of chargeback. The first is that the merchant should request authorization before every transaction naturally in accordance with the card company rules in order to process any transaction that is not authorized.

Another measure is to obtain authorization specifically at the rate and time of the transaction not long before it is not long after, long before it is risky because the authorization may expire in the meantime, in long after is useless because there was no authorization at the time of purchase. In finally not charging for elements such as dibs on a previously authorized amount, but instead of canceling the transaction and requesting authorization for a new one with the date included. For example, if they requested authorization for a $100 purchase and the person offers a 10% tip in the middle of it, they should not charge the $110 because the authorization is for $100.

They should avoid that transaction and request authorization for a new one with $110 value. What are some examples of the client or missing authorization? The first is a weak charge. Maybe the merchant obtains authorization from a consumer for a transaction, but then they wait a few days before actually processing the transaction and the authorization has expired in the meantime. The second example is what we just covered when the consumer offers a tip. Maybe the merchant, instead of requesting authorization for this new amount or nullifying the previous transaction, just charges it with a previous authorization which doesn't match. Finally, we have the example of lost or missing cards, which we'll take a look at later.

If a card is marked as lost or missing or in recovery by the card company. The reason code will be different, but the authorization will still be the client. It's a specific case of this type of situation. What are our key takeaways here? The first is that this type of reason code can be summarized as the merchant having processed a transaction for which they did not obtain authorization. Authorization is usually missing for the client. In other words, either the merchant was refused authorization or they didn't even bother to request it.

There may be multiple situations that lead to this, including an expiring authorization, additional transaction values such as trips or lost or stolen cards. So as we see this reason, code is used when the merchant doesn't have authorization or did not request for a specific amount. But remember, that doesn't mean that you don't have authorization in general. It just means that for this specific period of time for this specific value, they don't have authorization. So there are other problems which may be causing this.

Authorization: Card in Recovery/ Lost/Stolen

Let's talk about recent codes related to a credit card being lost, stolen or in recovery. That is, the person could have never authorized the transaction because they don't have the cards. It was lost, it was stolen or it was swallowed by an ATM, for example. And it's being recovered by the card company. Let's take a look. There is a group of reason codes that usually have to do with a card being reported to be lost, stolen or in recovery by the card company. The card may have been compromised in some way and it's either outside the card company's control or it's listed in a recovery bulletin.

So although this type of reason code may have some variations for different companies, the usual theme here is that due to the fact that the card has been reported as not being available to the cardholder, either because it's lost or stolen or in recovery, then regardless of reason, any transaction that uses this card should not be authorized. So when the merchant makes a request for authorization for the transaction, the answer will explicitly state that this card is in recovery or inaccessible.

Authorization will be declined. But more specifically stating this reason chargebacks of this type occur when the merchant disregards the response obtained and processes the transaction any way it's considered similar to the situation where authorization is declined in general. But in this case, it's for this specific reason that the card is not accessible to the cardholder. Some guidelines to avoid this type of situation include first, when the authorization request receives the client response, not processing the transaction basic in the above situation, optionally requesting an alternative method of payment for this transaction that is later hopefully authorized. Also following the acquirer banks guidelines in terms of what to do with cards that are reported stolen, lost or in recovery.

Also, when possible, avoiding manually inputting transactions because these are the errors, including possibly not acknowledging attack line authorization and also training internal staff so that they perform these actions as well and understand these nuances. What are some examples of situations where a card is in recovery, lost or stolen? The first is a lost card. If the merchant performs an authorization request on a card that is reported as lost, then authorization will be declined. This will be stated in the description if they process the transaction anyway, they're just asking for a chargeback. The second example is the same bit for a stolen car. So authorization is the client and it's stated that the card was stolen, but the merchant precedes anyway.

This is definitely going to lead to a chargeback later in. Finally, a card may be marked as in recovery by the card company. Or in other words, it has been lost, collected by an ATM machine, for example, and in the process of being routed to the card company, if that is the case, the authorization request will still be declined, but it'll mention that the card is in a recovery bulletin. So just like with other cases, if the merchant proceeds, you know what happens next? Chargeback. What are our key takeaways here? The first is that this group of reason codes occurs when authorization is required, but specifically for reasons related to the card being lost, stolen or in recovery.

There are three usual reasons for this, although the description may vary. The main reasons are that the cards are either stolen, lost or in recovery by the card company. And finally, merchants should be aware of the decline in authorization. This type of chargeback always happens because the merchant was the client authorized but decided to process the transaction anyway. So as we see, these are three distinct situations, but the key essence is the same. The person could have never authorized the transaction with the card because they don't have it at the end of the day.

Authorization: Invalid Information

Let's talk about invalid information reason codes. These usually occur when there is a problem with the card or the issuing bank. For example, you use a fake card on the point of sale, which is a fine and the authorisation is temporarily granted. But then after you've gone away and it connects to the Internet, you'll find out that the card was actually a fake. Let's take a look at this type of reason code besides the missing or the client authorization. It is possible to obtain authorization and still have it not be valid within the elaborate use usually has to do with invalid authorization information. There are multiple possible causes for this to happen. The first is an entry in what is called the warning bulletin of a card company.

In other words, when an authorization code has been transmitted but the issuing bank just can't confirm it. Usually due to a communication failure. Another example is when the account just doesn't exist. In other words, the issuing bank cannot find a valid account for the credit card number in the requested authorization. And finally, there are alternative or multiple authorization requests. For example, if authorization was an issue declined. But the merchant either keeps trying or uses another method for authorization, such as entering or voice authentication for the same transaction. Instead of creating a new one. Merchants can avoid this type of reason code in the following ways.

First, always requesting authorization before processing any transaction. That one is basic. Another method is closing the client transactions and opening new ones. Requesting an alternative method of payment for the new one. Instead of just trying to obtain a different authorization method for this same transaction that already includes the client authorization. In other words, not mixing things up. New authorization. New transaction. Another method is by being online as much as possible to prevent offline chip authorizations that may be from retired or false accounts. There's a type of fraud that precisely relies on using fraudulent credit cards while the person is in a flight for in-flight purchases.

The merchant will only realize that fraud when they come back down and they establish a connection to the network. It's also important to mention that a variation of this code occurs when authorization is provided for the wrong amount, when the transaction is beyond what is called the floor limit. The authorization naturally must be for the charged value. In this case, I'm not talking about a digit, such as charging 16 instead of $15. That's another reason to code a processing error for invalid amount. In this case, I'm talking about a completely different tier of price, such as charging $10,000 for a $10 purchase.

What are some examples of invalid information? The first are offline charges someone may use, as we just mentioned, a false credit card during a flight with a low amount in the point of sale will authorize it online and only realize the fraud when they come back down. And the authorization for that account later will not be found because the account never existed. Another example is a merchant that has their authorization declined but keeps trying over and over and uses alternative means, resulting in multiple attempts and possibly even multiple authorization types for one transaction which can cause invalid authorization information in finally, system or communication errors may result in authorization being provided but not communicated to the issuer in the eyes of the issuer.

This is considered invalid authorization as well. What are our key takeaways here? The first is that authorization information, besides being missing or declined, can actually be granted but still be incomplete or invalid. There are usually three main causes of invalid information, which are the issuer not receiving that information, missing account information or multiple authorization attempts. And finally, strong communication is a good guideline to solving all of these problems.

Although there are specific tactics, this type of chargeback can be prevented by constant incorrect communication of authorization information. So as we see this type of reason, code is raised when there is a problem with the account, with a card, or with the bank itself. And it's very common when there is no communication in real time, because there is no way to verify that something is fake.

Processing Errors: Introduction

Let's talk about processing error reason codes. These usually occur when there is a problem with the actual processing of a transaction. Wrong currency, wrong amount, wrong account, or many other types. Let's take a look. One category of chargeback reason codes has to do with what are called processing errors. These occur when a transaction is processed, but some of the information is wrong. In other words, the processing is just wrong. And this may be due to data related to the transaction amount, merchant codes, currencies or other invalid information.

There are also other types of processing errors that don't have to do with wrong data per say, but other processing problems such as duplicate transactions or transactions that were presented after an acceptable period. We are going to cover five key types of processing errors. The first reason is for invalid transaction codes or invalid data. These occur when transactions have the wrong transaction code or wrong data such as merchant name, merchant code or country within them. Then invalid amount or invalid account. Invalid amount occurs when the transaction amount does not correspond to the authorized one or the account does not correspond to the authorized one or doesn't exist then duplicate transactions or transactions paid by other means.

These occur when a payment has already been done or paid for other means. But this transaction is processed and it's a duplicate. After that, currency mismatches are very simple.

Either the merchant doesn't set the right currency in the transaction, doesn't set any currency, or they perform currency conversion without the cardholder's authorization. And finally, a way to present when the merchant takes too long to present the transaction. This can cause an error. So as you see in this group of topics, we are going to cover recent codes related to problems in the processing of the transaction itself.

Processing Errors: Invalid Code or Data

Let's cover two differences but related. Reason codes in invalid transaction code and invalid transaction data. Invalid transaction code relates to, for example, processing of debit instead of credit. That is, instead of, for example, charging you $20, giving you $20, all invalid transaction data has to do with wrong information about the merchant or transaction. For example, instead of being charged by Starbucks in the USA where you are, you are charged by Starbucks in the UK, for example. These two are different but related. Let's take a look. There is a group of reason codes that represent similar issues but are usually specified each with its own unique code. These are situations that involve invalid transaction codes and invalid transaction data.

Let me elaborate. First are invalid transaction codes. They simply occur when the transaction code provided was different from the real one. So the merchant process, a credit transaction instead of a debit one or processed the transaction in some other way, that is different from the transaction described in the authorization requested. So there is a mismatch about the specific transaction type. The second is valid transaction data. This is when the merchant submits an authorization request that contains incorrect information such as having the wrong merchant code, country merchant or transaction type or others. When this type of situation occurs, the merchant usually has to void the transaction and accept the dispute and if possible, create a new transaction with the correct information.

It can be prevented by. First of all, double checking all data sounds, including the most frequently mistyped Data, which may be the name of your city state, actual merchant name or others. And now the recommendation is to always include all necessary information. Missing information can be considered invalid as well, and merchants should always train their staff to perform these checks as well so that everyone does it. What are some examples of invalid transaction codes or data? The first is an invalid MTC or merchant category code. Ironically, the merchant may make the mistake of getting their own merchant code wrong. Even if this authorization is granted, the data will be invalid. Another example are the small, quick mistakes that merchants can make.

It's very common for someone to make a small mistake here or there, such as entering one digit wrong or one way or wrong and compromising the transaction code, merchant code or another field. And finally, there is no guarantee that you can avoid this type of chargeback, but it all begins by training staff to diligently double check transaction data. Doing this already goes a long way. What are our key takeaways? The first is that one type of reason code will occur when the transaction code itself is wrong. Processing a debit instead of a credit, a credit instead of a rebuttal, and so on.

The second is that transaction data itself can be wrong, wrong merchant code, location, transaction ID and so on. And the reason code will be a distinct one from this other situation in finally paying attention helps. These situations are almost always generated by human error. So a chance on the part of the merchants goes a long way in preventing them from sending wrong information in the first place. So as we see these two reasons codes are different but related, there is a problem with the code of the transaction or the data of the transaction. And at the end of the day, the only way to prevent them is to pay attention and be diligent to not make mistakes.

Processing Errors: Invalid Amount/ Account

Talk about the reason COATES for involving a mount for involving the count. These are different but again related invalid. The mount has to do with charging you a different amount than the one that was authorized. An invalid account is all about charging the wrong person. The person who is not involved with the transaction itself wins the goal. There are two types of processing errors that may occur, and they have to do with having incorrect information either relating to the transaction amount or the transaction account. So there are usually two distinct reason codes. The first type of situation is when the transaction amount is incorrect or invalid.

This usually occurs when the transaction amount does not match the one in the authorization request. It's somewhat frequent when merchants type numbers themselves. So you may have authorization for the 21.34 transaction, but you charge 21.43 or you may change the digit. The second example is having an incorrect or invalid account number, or in other words, this occurs when the account number in the transaction does not match the one in the authorization. The account number may be incorrectly entered, or it may be a case of an adjustment where the account is closed or has no chance when the transaction is processed and is therefore considered an invalid account.

In both cases, many of these chargebacks can be prevented by the merchant just checking transaction information before processing it. For this specific case of invalid account numbers, there are additional recommendations because these may be due to wrong information, but also actual authentication problems. So first, merchants should always swipe or insert this physical card for payment. Any other methods of using the card that does not include the chip or the magnetic strip is not recommended when the terminal cannot leave the magnetic strip or trip of a card. An authorization should be requested by the team in the account number or calling to obtain authorization approval.

And when that authorization is granted, the authorization code should be carefully typed on the sales receipt. When requesting the secondary payment method, be aware of any payment method whose member visits match the card's one. So if you obtain an off reservation for a payment and the person wants to use a different car, any accident to use their company card is that of their personal card, which the authorization was for. That is going to result in a chargeback with an invalid account. Reason There is any variation of the invalid amount in code, which is usually represented by its own code, which corresponds to an invalid installment.

This usually occurs naturally in payments with multiple installments, and it occurs when the cardholder claims that a merchant either charged the wrong installment or at the time is with the other invalid amount situations that can be prevented by the merchant double checking any transaction, including the amount that was charged as well and the timing of that transaction. For example, if the right installment is charged to one week, for example, at the beginning of the month instead of the end of the month, then is enough to cause a chargeback. What are some examples looking around amounts or accounts? The first is a transaction amount.

This can occur especially when typing amounts by hand. In one digit is enough to have the wrong account number or the wrong amount, which leads to a chargeback. The second example is having multiple payment methods. If authorization is requested for a payment method, but the cardholder asks to use a different one, it's important to make sure if the account number is not different. Otherwise, there is going to be a problem. The example if you just mention a person's personal account and company account and finally mistaken digits can be another problem, whether with transaction amounts or with account numbers.

Typing things by hand in means typing a digit can happen to any merchant and this invalidates authorization and will cause a subsequent chargeback. What are our key takeaways here? Is that chargebacks within valid amount reason codes occur when the charge the miles does not correspond to the one used in the authorization request. So you have permission to charge some amount. Different one chargebacks with an invalid account reason could occur when the account number information for the transaction doesn't match the one in the authorization request. So you have permission to charge a certain account, but you charge a different one.

And finally, as with many other reason codes, most chargebacks of this nature can be prevented by simply double checking the information before processing transactions to make sure that there are no mistakes in the numbers. So as we see, these are two different but related reason codes. Invalid amount is also charged a different amount than the one that was authorized. Well, it is always the count that is all about charging the wrong person, which is a bit scary if you think about it. And as with other reason codes, the best way to fix it is to pay attention and not make mistakes in the first place.

Processing Errors: Duplicate/Other Payment

Let's talk about two duplicate transactions or transactions paid by other means. What the reason codes mean is the following. When you pay for a transaction, either it's a duplicate because you've already paid for that product or you've paid for other means. For example, you give $20 in cash, but you are still charged $20 on your cards. These are different, but again, related. Let's take a look at this type of chargeback in reason could occur when a single transaction is processed two or more times or when a transaction is processed that was paid through other means. In short, for one reason or another, the composer is not supposed to be for this transaction, or it's not supposed to exist because they have already paid in some other form.

There may be multiple causes for this code, but frequently the merchant batches multiple transactions at once, which may contain duplicates and they don't double check or they are processing transactions. It would already be like other means and they don't remember it or don't verify it before processing this transaction. This type of chargeback can usually be avoided with a set of precautions on the merchant's part. First, making sure to review batched transactions before executing them to make sure to enter or correct. So if you have a list of 50 transactions, don't just blindly process all of them, make sure every single one is valid and make sure to review all transaction receipts before posting them with the parent similar to the previous one.

Also diligently identifying and avoiding duplicate transactions which is achieved by the previous two, but also by being attentive to detail then not depositing the transaction with more than one acquiring bank. This actually happens. So a merchant will have one transaction, but they have two bank accounts. So they process the transaction for each one of their bank accounts in duplicate. Another is not mistaken when creating two receipts or mistaking both copies of the sales receipt. For example, the merchant copy and the sales copy for two transactions. So a merchant might take two different versions of the same copy and think that they are two different transactions.

And finally, training their staff to also perform all of these actions. What are some examples of duplicate payments or payments paid by other means? The first is having two receipts for two banks in case the merchant has two or more bank accounts. They may make the mistake of depositing a transaction with both banks, resulting in a duplicate. Another example is someone having already paid. Maybe the merchant uses one major invoicing system, but a client has already paid for an invoice using other means. So it's outside the system, if you will, and the merchant is not aware of this in charging that again through the system. I've had this happen to me myself a long time ago. Most of my clients would pay for Stripe, but once one client decided to pay for a bank transfer and it didn't tell me.

So I actually thought that they didn't pay for Stripe and charge them again. This is an example of how this can happen in an economy . A mistake in the merchant copy in the sales copy is another mistake. These are two versions of sales copy based on this same sales draft. These are for the same transaction. But in merchants there is this attractive or handsome experience that can mistake them for two distinct transactions and effectively duplicate it. What are our key takeaways here? The first is that this type of reason code describes a situation in which the client has already paid for a transaction somehow. So this one is either a duplicate or it's not needed. Then duplicates occur.

One of the major reasons for this is that codes implicates either depositing the transaction in two different banks or considering that two seats are two transactions when therefore the same one or other variations. And finally, diligent reviews help. Although it's not always possible to detect this type of mistake if the merchant again increases their team to be as well, they can greatly decrease the chances of this occurring. So as we see these two types of situations are different but related, it means that the person has already paid for this transaction. In the past, either by other means or they have literally paid for it. And you are charging them again. As with many other reason codes, the best way to not fall into this trap is to pay attention in the first place.

Processing Errors: Currency Mismatches

Let's talk about currency mismatches. These reason codes include problems with the actual currency of the transaction. For example, you agree to be charged $100, but you pay €100 or you agree to pay $100. But the conversion rate used is one that's very different to the one which you agree to wait. Sticker shock. There is a group of recent codes that relates to mismatches in the currency use. These usually have three major reasons represented by the same reason. The first is a different currency. So the merchant simply used a different currency than the one authorized for the transaction. For example, having authorization to charge $10 in charging €10.

The second example is having an invalid currency. So the merchant didn't provide the currency or provide valid currency information. So in the same example above, they have permission to charge $10 and try to charge ten. Maybe the default currency is used or a different one. That was not planned. And lastly, there is a possible disagreement over dynamic currency conversion. That is, the merchant may have decided to use dynamic currency conversion, but the cardholder may not have agreed to this or if he's involved in it. If you've ever tried to make a payment in a different currency and the website shows you exactly what the conversion is, what the rate is, and what the fee is.

And you have to click the checkbox, for example. Now they are trying to avoid precisely this. There are multiple measures that merchants can take to both deal with this type of code and prevent it. First, they should inform their consumers of the currency being used or currency conversion practices which ever apply here as well as the fees involved before the purchase. This should be done very explicitly. Then, when the consumer has agreed with the currency or the currency conversion use, the merchant should provide proof of that. To resolve the dispute. Naturally, they have to show that the consumer bequeathed it. The merchant should always provide the consumer the possibility of paying in their local currency.

Because this causes a lot less misunderstandings. It may not be an issue, for example, between dollars in euros, but in a currency where one of them is the 100th or 1000 of another currency, it can become an issue. And finally, the merchant should train their staff in terms of how to deal with transactions that involve the different currencies. What are some examples of currency mismatches? The first is the simple mismatch of a symbol using the wrong currency during a transaction. A merchant that charges €500 would have authorization for $500 then not having agreement in terms of currency. The merchant charges for a purchase and converts from the consumer's local currency, but they do not warn them on the fees involved or maybe even the rate used.

And finally, not actually providing a currency is another example. The merchant may simply forget to provide the currency use so the transaction will have no currency data or resume of the fault. It may be different. What are our key takeaways here? The first is that this type of reason quote occurs when the merchant provides the wrong currency. No currency or any currency date has not been agreed upon because due to conversion issues, maybe the merchant decided to perform currency conversion, but the consumer simply did not agree to it. And finally, this can be avoided by practicing, quote unquote, good currency hygiene.

In short, entering currencies correctly in obtaining cardholder confirmation on which to use or dynamic conversion if it's the case and always having proof of it. So as we see these reason codes occur when there is a problem with the currency or the conversion rate. And the best way to prevent them is to very explicitly give a person to agree to the currency and the conversion rate before the transaction.

Processing Errors: Late Presentment

Let's talk about late resentment, reason codes. And the rationale for these is very simple. The merchants and it's a transaction after too much time has actually passed. For example, a client bought something yesterday, but it took two months to process that transaction and send it to the bank. Let's take a look. This reason code usually has one very simple reason the transaction was not sent to the bank or the card processor. Within the required time limit. There are usually time limits for both the issuing bank and the acquirer bank to receive the transaction. The latter are usually much shorter because the acquirer bank is the one that represents the merchant.

This type of chargeback occurs when the merchant doesn't share transaction information in a timely manner. The variation of this occurs when the account of the merchant or cardholder is not in good standing by the time that the transaction is processed. For example, the consumer makes a purchase and spends all their money the next day in the transaction. This process after that when there is no money in the account. This may occur in cases of fraud. In this case, the merchant is not necessarily late, but they're late enough for the account to have changed conditions which renders the transaction invalid.

In order to avoid this type of problem in the future, merchants simply need to communicate completed transactions to their cards, processor or merchant bank as soon as possible. It's not possible for all merchants, especially those with global operations, but it should be done as much as possible to minimize risk as much as possible. The ideal is to send them within 24 hours. But in many cases the problem isn't just forgetfulness, right? It may be the case that the merchant gets the actual account number wrong. This forces them to send the transaction to avoid it, correct it, and then send it again later.

In this case, it may be the second version that is linked, just like a child who is doing their homework. You get it wrong, you have to fix it and have to redo it again before the deadline. But that doesn't matter because the deadline doesn't change on the cardholder side. It's impossible to guarantee that the account will be in good standing by the time that the transaction goes through. You just expect it to be. But again, this can be minimized by merchants communicating transactions as soon as possible. What are some examples of late presentment situations? The first is a forgotten transaction for big businesses that combined multiple occasions.

It is frequent for transactions to be group intended positive later, but if they're late enough, the consumer may have forgotten about the transaction and they don't recognize it or something may even happen to their account. In the meantime, as mentioned, it is possible for this weakness to be due to incorrect numbers. The merchant may give an account number wrong or misreported to their bank, which causes incomplete authorization and then some meaning. The transaction takes time. Another aspect is the merchant agreement. The specific line at Bankstown, particularly the one in the merchant bank, has for their merchant clients to submit transactions, is unique in its stated in their specific merchant agreement.

What are our key takeaways here? The first is that late presentment chargeback reason codes, and the simple reason is that the transaction was presented for processing too late. This may happen for maybe the reasons. It may be that the merchant bought an account number wrong and they have to resubmit it, which makes it late. Or it may happen because they just forgot to submit it. There are specific deadlines which are fact presented by merchants in the one that their merchant bank imposes on them. He's one of these. So as we see, there may be many reasons for why a transaction is presented to weight problems with the account. The deadline is too short for others. But what this reason code symbolizes at the end of the day, is that the transaction was presented too late.

Consumer Disputes: Introduction

Our last category of reason Codes for Chargebacks is related to consumer disputes. There is no formal error, but the consumer claims that something is different to what it actually is, a counterfeit product, a discount which was not applied and more. Let's take a look. As the name implies, chargebacks that are due to consumer disputes have to do with differences of expectations between the consumer and the merchant usually occur when there is a legitimate problem with a product which can range from defaults to misrepresentation to allegations of the product being counterfeit to the product not being delivered.

But also when there is consumer fraud besides issues with products or services, these disputes also occur when there are issues with payments such as consumers being charged for products that they didn't use or not having receipts, credit that is due to them. We are going to cover three key types of consumer disputes. The first is a mismatch of goods. Differences in expectations between the consumer and the merchant relative to the products that were provided. Maybe there are perceived defects, non-delivery, or others. The second type of reason codes are related to transactions that were canceled or not completed.

In short, you don't complete a transaction, but you are charged for it anyway, or you cancel it. But that is not registered in the merchant system. And finally, credit not processed is a reason codes dealing with consumer credit not being processed either totally or partially. So as we see this group of topics which we're going to cover a reason codes related to any type of dispute or misunderstanding between the merchant and the person who purchased the product.

Consumer Disputes: Mismatch of Goods

Let's talk about recent coats related to a mismatch in goods. That is a person bought something but it's not what they thought or at least that's what they claim. This type of reason code can be valid or not because the consumer themselves may be lying to commit fraud. Let's take a look. There are a variety of reasons, codes that are related to consumer disputes. It's then in particular from there being a mismatch between the goods presented and the goods receipt. It can include, for example, first defective or misrepresented goods. This occurs when the consumer claims that the goods are not a state, so usually goods of lower quality or that they are defective in some way and therefore they ask for the money back.

Another possibility is a non-delivery of goods. So the consumer claims that the goods were simply not delivered. This may be true or a case of a consumer from another possibility claiming that the goods are counterfeit. So the consumer claims that the goods that they receive are not the present products but counterfeit copies. It's important to know that all of these variations of this reason code may be legitimate or there may be fraud. I'm part of the consumer. So they may be lying just to get the money back. So both can and do occur frequently. It's usually the merchant documentation that decides these disputes.

In these cases, some recommendations for the merchant include providing honesty in details, product descriptions, to make sure that expectations are aligned from the beginning, then making sure that the right products are shipped. If this happens, the wrong product is sent, namely inferior ones, and naturally a chargeback will occur. Also, if the merchant promptly accepts returns and issues credit for consumers, if the conditions for such do apply in that they certify the authenticity of the goods, specifically for the case of allegations of the products being counterfeit. What are some examples of mismatches of goods? The first are counterfeit goods. Some consumers may purchase a product that upon reception, they verified as a fake.

This is frequent for consumer electronics, such as iPhones or gaming consoles like PlayStations. It's also frequent, however, for consumers to claim that the product is counterfeit in order to return it after using it. An example of these disputes is what is called satisfaction from. This is a type of fraud which consists of using a product and then returning it or claiming it to be of low quality. It's frequent with movies, video games or similar products. And finally, the consumer may claim that the goods have not been delivered when they have. This is a type of fraud called non-delivery trouble, and it's frequent to be avoided by the merchant, either using fraud monitoring techniques such as shipping, address verification, or just using transporters that document the delivery in detail.

What are our key takeaways here? The first is that there are multiple variations in recent codes, but what these have in common is that there is a mismatch between the seller and the consumer's perceptions and expectations. Then it's all about showing proof. The merchant showing proof is essential to dispute the chargeback proof that the product was on the scribe, that it's authentic in its delivery and so on. And finally, this type of dispute can be legitimate or fraudulent. A product may really not match the expectations of a consumer, or the dispute may be false with the consumer committing fraud.

So as we see this type of reason code or multiple reason codes may be raised when there is some sort of mismatch in expectations about a product, it may be counterfeit, it may be of lower quality, never have been the way and so on. But it's important to note that it may be true, it may be the actual merchant's fault, or it may just be the consumer trying to commit fraud.

Consumer Disputes: Canceled/Not Completed

Let's talk about canceled or not completed transactions. Reason goes as the name says, this reason code is raised when a transaction was not completed which was charged anyway or when it was authorized, but it was canceled afterwards, which was still charged. It's very common with subscription products. You cancel, but then you're still charged. Let's think about this group of reasons. Codes usually have in common the fact that a transaction was not authorized by the consumer. And there are usually two major causes to this. The first is that the transaction was canceled, so the consumer may place the transaction, but they canceled it in the meantime and they were charged anyway.

This also occurs frequently with recurring subscriptions that are canceled while they are still charged. The second variation is that the transaction was incomplete, so the consumer may have provided a part of the information or all of the necessary information to complete a purchase, but they never actually buy. And guess what? They were charged anyway. This also occurs when goods are not used, but they aren't charged for, for example, newspaper consumption. And the merchant provides you with the next batch. But they never warn you, you never use it, and you get charged for it anyway.

Merchants can avoid this type of dispute with consumers by, first of all, processing, cancellation and refund requests as soon as possible and warning the customer when these are processed, then clearly warning consumers about return in cancellation policies from the get go. Also always confirming transactions by email and the rest masse so that the consumer is always aware whether they occurred or not. Also always warning consumers when credit has been issued for return or that a cancellation occurred so that they have confirmation of it.

Also always terminating recurring transactions when requested by the consumer in finally never prematurely billing the cardholder, especially for subscriptions or for products or services that have not been consumed yet. What are some examples of cancel or not complete transactions? The first is a subscription charge. If the subscription service is shady, they may charge a person before the due date, which makes it even worse if the person cancels what is charged for the next period anyway. Another example are rate return policies. A merchant may not be clear on return policies, which may lead consumers to cancel a purchase or return it, only to find out that it's not possible and not even know why. And finally, treaty trial periods, quote unquote, are another example.

There are some mobile applications that offer a trial period coupled with a subscription. In other words, it's not really a trial period. You are committing to the first month with the seven days included. So consumers that are not aware of this will expect no charge because they believe it is a trial period. But then they're going to find out that there is one. What are our key takeaways here? The first is that the common element with these recent codes is that this charge is not supposed to happen because either the transaction was canceled or it was never complete in the first place. One reason for this is code on canceled transactions that are not processed either because there's not a clear cancellation policy or the merchant just forgot to cancel them or they do not want to know.

The reasons are incomplete transactions where the consumer thinks that they are not being charged yet because they haven't reached that stage. But guess what? They aren't charged. So as we see, there may be many multiple reasons for this code, the transaction may have never been completed or it was completed and canceled. But at the end of the day, when the charge occurred, there was no reason to charge the person.

Consumer Disputes: Credit Not Processed

Whites coverage credit not processed reason goes this type of reason goes because when you were supposed to obtain a discount or you have an amount in credit, but that amount is not considered or even worse, when you were supposed to receive a quantity on your part, but instead you are charged that amount, which is a nightmare. Let's take a look at this type of reason. This type of chargeback occurs in three major different situations that have to do with a consumer having credit. That is not a process. The first is when credit is not processed on time. For example, the merchant has agreed to an amount of credit for the consumer, but it has not been processed yet. They tell you to use $20 credit in our store, which you never end up receiving.

It may occur because the merchant is late or because they don't agree with the credit and refuse to actually process it. Another possibility is that credit is not fully processed during an actual purchase, so a consumer makes a purchase. Applying an amount of credit in some of it or all of it does not apply. For example, you are offered $100 credit in the retailer and you find out that you can only use 80 or that it's not even accepted in the first place. And finally, the credit is processed as a debit for sale. So instead of processing a certain amount of debit for a consumer they are charged with, that amount is a nightmare scenario.

So you are told that you get $50 in credit and you find out that not only did you not get them, which you were charged with those $50, it's that if you're paying attention, you may also realize that this can be a type of processing error within a valid transaction code, because instead of a credit it was processed. And to have it faced with this type of situation, merchants should take measures such as first processing all requests for credit as soon as possible when advising customers or what the credit amount will be, as well as the timeline for its reception and training of merchant staff to properly process grab it so that it's not accidentally processed as a debit or a sale.

It's very possible that in this type of situation, the merchant is being fraudulent on purpose. But more frequently than not, this is simply the result of carelessness or innocent merchant error. It's not usually on purpose. What are some examples of credits not processed? The first example is serving -$20 instead of plus two. A consumer buys a book for $20 and asks for the money back, but instead of receiving $20 in credit, they are charged again for 20 hours. So the credit was processed as part of it. Another example is credit not being fully provided.

So a consumer has $10 in credit, but they find out that only eight of those loans have been applied because there is a specific fee and they have not been informed of this. Another example is waiting on credit. So a consumer may have received a green light from a merchant to receive $50 in credit, but they may have been waiting for months without obtaining it. What are our key takeaways? The first is that this type of reason code usually pertains to situations where a consumer should have received credit, but they haven't, or possibly even charged for that credit. There are three major forms of this type of dispute.

Either the credit has not been provided by the merchant or it has been only partially provided or it was actually charged instead of credit. And finally, the best way for merchants to avoid this type of thorny situation is to clarify with consumers the amounts and timeframes of credit provided in different situations. So as we see this reason, code occurs when the person has a discount or an amount in credit which is not applied or even worse, they're charged that amount and there's no way to prevent it except to be very explicit about what credit or discount they are supposed to get and whether it will be applied in this transaction or not. And what are they going to be charged in this transaction?

Conclusion

We are now at the end of the Chargeback Reason Codes chapter. Let's take a moment just to recap the four categories of recent codes as well as consolidate your knowledge with some questions. With this, we close the charge panic quiz and quotes chapter. Our goal in this chapter was to cover the different types of reason codes for chargebacks by holders or their issuing banks. In order to achieve this, we covered the four main types of reason codes for chargebacks. The first was from disputes raised due to quant merchants, stolen or lost cards or EMV transactions gone wrong in authorization issues, transactions processed by merchants having been declined authorization, not having requested it in the first place, or having invalid authorization information then processing errors.

Transactions processed with wrong codes, wrong data, or to wait, among other problems. And finally, consumer disputes. Disputes due to customer perception, including issues over product quality and finished transactions being charged or credit not being processed. What are some questions that you can ask yourself to consolidate the content in this chapter? The first is what are the three types of issues that may occur when processing the customers? Whose liability is it when an EMV transaction is not being properly processed? The card companies or the merchants? Out of curiosity, whose liability is it when an EMV transaction has been perfectly processed.

What category does a currency mismatch belong to? What is this fraudulent processing system and how does it differ from an invalid amount transaction? What are some problems that may occur with receiving goods that consumers may have at rates? Give me one or two examples. What are three situations where a card is not available to the cardholder but is still used fraudulently? With this, we closed the chargeback Reason Codes chapter where we try to cover the major categories of reason, codes and chargebacks as well as the most common types of reason codes within each.

Final Words

We are now at the end of the introduction to dispute resolution cause we've covered it a lot. Reason codes, IVR, OCR, Merchant Banks and more. Wait, stick a moment. Just to recap the main chapters of this Book, we are now at the end of the introduction to this resolution Book. From this Book, we aim to cover the essentials of dispute resolution, especially in payment disputes involving merchants and cardholders with expert topics such as how ADR or alternative dispute resolution differs from litigation as well as the different implementations of it. Then what the OCR or Open Dispute Resolution Framework consists of, as well as its main principles and implementations.

Then we covered how dispute resolution works for merchant clients by acquiring or merchant banks, including the dispute lifecycle, the scheme involvement and general guidelines. And finally, we covered the usual reason codes for chargebacks from issuing banks, as well as what measures merchants should take in the face of each. To achieve this, we covered four chapters total. The first were approaches to ADR negotiation, mediation or arbitration, the pros and cons and implementations up. Then we covered the OCR framework, what it consists of and how it's implemented.

Then we covered dispute resolution in merchant banking, the usual process that a dispute follows the general guidelines and conditions for a possible scheme involvement. Finally, we covered specific reason codes for chargebacks by issuing banks what each type of reason code means, as well as what merchants should do in the face of each witness. We close the introduction to the Dispute Resolution Book. I hope that this Book has taught you more about dispute resolution, especially for payment disputes, and that it has helped you professionally. Thank you so much for reading. With this, we close the introduction to the dispute resolution Book. Thank you so much for reading.

Don't miss out!

Visit the website below and you can sign up to receive emails whenever Book Wave Publications publishes a new book. There's no charge and no obligation.

https://books2read.com/r/B-A-LAFAB-MVMTC

BOOKS 2 READ

Connecting independent readers to independent writers.

Also by Book Wave Publications

How To Make Money In Stocks Value Investing Strategies
Master The Steps To Move Away From The Past And
Following Inspiration
Heartful Journeys: Exploring The Power Of Mindful Living
Essential Computer Networking Concepts You Should Know
Harnessing Your Inner Strength Overcoming Limiting Beliefs
Mastering Networking Basics From Novice To Pro
Mastering Success Harnessing The Hidden Potential Of
Presuppositions
Start Your Own Business, Be Your Own Boss
Passive Income Powerhouse Learn To Set Yourself Up For Life
PCI DSS Bootcamp The A-Z Information Security Guide